Praise for *Step Out of Your Story*

"This book presents many helpful ideas with clarity and humor. There is something for every individual seeking the golden thread or 'yellow brick road' that leads from suffering to joy and from pain to spiritual health."

— **Nancy Rosanoff**, spiritual counselor and author of *Intuition Workout*

"Our life histories shape us, our attitudes, our life views, and our relationships as well as our strengths and weaknesses. Kim Schneiderman's book is a fantastic demonstration of this."

— **Samuel C. Klagsbrun, MD**, executive medical director, Four Winds Hospital

"Read this ingeniously devised book, do the exercises, and discover how you can step out of your story and take control of your life."

— **Albert J. Bernstein, PhD**, author of *Dinosaur Brains* and *Emotional Vampires*

"*Step Out of Your Story* is a truly fresh approach to reflective writing. By placing our own lives in the context of plotlines, characters, and narrative devices, Kim Schneiderman provides an ingenious way to twist our culture's fascination with reality TV and sensational movies and channel it toward the story that matters most: the narrative of our own lives. Both entertaining and evocative, this book's approach to self-awareness promises to reveal a fascinating story you may not have realized was inside you."

— **Marney K. Makridakis**, author of *Creating Time* and *Hop, Skip, Jump*

"In *Step Out of Your Story*, Kim Schneiderman shows us in step-by-step, practical, and creative exercises how to change our lives by changing our stories. What an innovative way to channel our natural storytelling abilities into a powerful ally for a richer, more satisfying life."

— **Judy Reeves**, author of *Wild Women, Wild Voices*

STEP OUT
of Your Story

WRITING EXERCISES TO
REFRAME AND TRANSFORM
YOUR LIFE

Kim Schneiderman, LCSW, MSW

New World Library
Novato, California

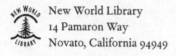

 New World Library
14 Pamaron Way
Novato, California 94949

Text design by Tona Pearce Myers and Tracy Cunningham
Plot diagram that first appears on page 20 by Tracy Cunningham

Library of Congress Cataloging-in-Publication Data
Schneiderman, Kim, date.
Step out of your story : writing exercises to reframe and transform your life / Kim Schneiderman, LCSW, MSW
    pages cm
Includes bibliographical references.
ISBN 978-1-60868-232-4 (paperback) — ISBN 978-1-60868-233-1 (ebook)
1. Narrative therapy. 2. Psychotherapy—Problems, exercises, etc. 3. Personal construct therapy. I. Title.
RC489.S74S36 2015
616.89'165—dc23   2015010467

First printing, June 2015
ISBN 978-1-60868-232-4
Printed in Canada on 100% postconsumer-waste recycled paper

New World Library is proud to be a Gold Certified Environmentally Responsible Publisher. Publisher certification awarded by Green Press Initiative. www.greenpressinitiative.org

10   9   8   7   6   5   4   3   2

To my parents, Linda and Bernie Schneiderman,
who live on through the stories we tell about them

CONTENTS

PREFACE: MY STORY

*What matters in life is not what happens to you, but what you
remember and how you tell it.*

— Gabriel García Márquez, *Gabriel Living to Tell the Tale*

When I was a little girl, I used to sign my name "Kim
S., in person." Between my highly active imagination, my obsession with Nancy Drew books, and my daily diet of television, I had the uncanny sense that I was a character in a story. I
couldn't exactly say why or who was watching. Perhaps it was
because of my well-meaning but marginally overbearing parents or the inflated sense of self-importance that afflicts many
would-be writers who imagine themselves as the stars of their
own terribly compelling dramas.

My sense of being a character, though tempered by maturity, followed me into adulthood, where I kept it under wraps, while secretly turning to my "Kim S." alter ego in times of stress. Whenever I had a "why me?" moment — times when I felt victimized by difficult people or circumstances — I'd imagine reading about the exact same situation in a novel. First, I would ask myself, "What would I hope the main character would do in response to these circumstances? What actions or outcomes would I root for as the reader of this story?" Second, because I appreciate good character development in novels, I'd wonder, "Why would a benevolent author place this character in this particular situation?" And, "What might this situation be teaching her?" Finally, because I see life as a spiritual story that I'm coauthoring: "How might she make the most of this situation to become a stronger, more compassionate human being?"

The answers to these questions and similar lines of inquiry helped me successfully navigate many challenging chapters in my life, emerging from them as a stronger, wiser, and happier person. Enhanced by my insights as a psychotherapist and journalist, such questions became the basis for a series of writing workshops I began offering around the New York metropolitan area in 2008. My hope was that self-exploratory writing in the third-person voice could help participants — many of whom had been impacted by the recession — reframe their losses as stepping-stones to a richer spiritual life and a deeper sense of self.

Like the protagonist in many stories, my Pollyannish premise was soon put to the test. In February 2012, my seventy-two-year-old father developed an aggressive form of cancer that took his life a few months later. Suddenly, I was a single, middle-aged orphan. My father's death was the third cancer fatality in my small, immediate family in seven years. In 2005, my sixty-one-year-old mother lost her decade-long battle with ovarian cancer. Less than a year later, my father found love again. Four years later, his girlfriend died after a year-long battle with lung cancer, also at sixty-one.

After experiencing so many devastating losses, I had to ask myself, "Could I walk my talk? Did I truly believe that I had the power to transform my tragedies into triumphs simply by choosing to widen the lens through which I viewed my own story?"

Yes, I did, but understanding how requires reading between the lines. My father was the antagonist of my childhood story. The external narrative — how it looked from the outside — was that he was a good provider who worked tirelessly to offer his children all the opportunities he had been denied growing up in a working-class Jewish family in the Bronx. Yet the internal story, how I experienced him, was quite different. I never felt he understood me. He was a benevolent despot of sorts, and his "because I told you so" was never a satisfying response to all my important "why" questions. Because I was equally headstrong, I challenged him, and I made my mother my confidante. When I graduated college, I moved to San Francisco, putting several cities and mountain ranges between us.

Yet our story took an unexpected, positive turn after my mother died and I moved back to New York. Suddenly, my father and I were spending more time together, grieving my mother over Chinese food, biking up northern Westchester trails, sharing our mutual love of dance, and flying to California for family gatherings. I was older and wiser, and having undergone years of therapy, I had come to appreciate my father's many positive attributes without taking his rougher edges quite so personally.

It wasn't until my father suddenly became ill that our father-daughter narrative reached its inevitable climax.

It's December 2011. My father, who has recently moved to Florida, has just been transferred from intensive care to a hospice unit at Delray Medical Center, less than a mile from his new home in Boca Raton. The admitting nurse explains that he needs twenty-four-hour supervision to receive services at home. My brother is immersed in a rigorous master's program at Cornell University. I have been my father's primary health advocate for the past three months, flying back and forth between my life in New York and Florida. Hiring a full-time aide is not only unaffordable, it's also unthinkable.

So I decide to take a leave of absence — from my private practice, my friends, my community, and my frenetic but full life in Manhattan — to care for my father. It's been eighteen years since we lived under the same roof; the last time, he was my provider. Now, the tables are not only turned, they are covered with painkiller cocktails, Ensure, and a stockpile of sweets. Over the next two months, I fix his meals, administer his meds, clean his house, learn to manage his finances, and hold his hand, both figuratively and literally, through waves of fear and pain.

Despite the stress, which I alleviate with exercise and beach walks, I feel my heart softening and expanding. My father and I share surprising moments of tears and laughter. We come to appreciate each other's minds, feelings, and strengths more deeply. Old friends and family show up to talk about the good old times, offer support, and say their good-byes. I reconnect with long-lost relatives and see how fortunate I am to have such a supportive community of friends and family.

As this new and final chapter in our story continues to cook us, all our oniony father-daughter pungency melts into sweetness. One evening, my father tells me that, despite his fear and misery, he can't believe he is still learning and growing. I ask what he means, and he responds, "That people have found a way to love me and that I have found a way to love them." That's all he ever wanted. That's all anyone ever wants, isn't it?

Today, I realize there are many ways to spin my story. Mine is but one version; others might tell it differently. As both the narrator and protagonist of my narrative, I exercise my authorship rights to tell it as a story of love and redemption...of the prodigal daughter, perhaps.

I also recognize that not all stories end in redemption. There is a place in this world for sadness. The more tragic the event, the more difficult it can be to put our faith in an empowering narrative. Some events — war, genocide, terrorism, disease, poverty — can lead us to question the stories we've always taken for granted. They defy the comforting plotlines or the preexisting narratives we have created about divinity, humanity, and justice. Had I been given a choice, I would have chosen another storyline and resolution for my life's lessons. But for now, I embrace the gifts of my bittersweet fortune.

That's my story, and I'm sticking to it.

INTRODUCTION

> *We tell ourselves stories in order to live.... We interpret what
> we see, select the most workable of the multiple choices. We live
> entirely...by the imposition of a narrative line upon disparate
> images, by the "ideas" with which we have learned to freeze
> the shifting phantasmagoria — which is our actual experience.*
> — Joan Didion, *The White Album*

Sometimes the story of your life reads like a comedy; other times, like a tragedy. But if you read the text through the proper lens, you can always read your story as a personal growth adventure.

This book is built around a series of structured writing exercises designed to help you reimagine yourself as the hero of your unfolding story with the power to reclaim your personal narrative through choice and voice.

1

As a psychotherapist, former journalist, and consummate seeker, I offer you a framework, tools, and insights gleaned from both sides of the therapy couch. My aim is to help you respond to all the moving pieces in your life so that they conspire to help grow the best possible version of yourself — I want to help you to play your best role, so to speak, in the story of your life, your family, your society, and perhaps even the world.

To do this, I will guide you in applying classic storytelling elements to your own life, using the third-person narrative to elevate your perspective. This is not just a gimmick; rather, it's a therapeutic technique inspired by a growing body of research that shows that viewing your life as an objective observer can help you see yourself through gentler, more compassionate eyes. It is also aligned with narrative therapy techniques that put emotional distance between people and their storylines so they don't overidentify with their problems.

My book doesn't follow any single ideology. Rather, it is a carefully constructed stew of ideas, consisting of several parts psychology; a few heaping tablespoons of Buddhism, Kabbalah, and Mussar (a nineteenth-century Jewish character development program); a dash of very basic literary theory; and a sprinkle of imagination sifted through my life-long fascination with human potential.

This method presumes that a) telling our story is a fundamental way that we come to know ourselves and make meaning of our lives; and b) how we "read," or rather interpret, our story affects how we feel about ourselves, which can influence how our lives unfold. For example, if we tell the story of a cancer diagnosis as a tale of finding new sources of resilience and deeper connections with loved ones, this feels very different from telling the story as one of divine punishment or meaningless misery. In concrete terms, a positive narrative can influence prognosis, as study after study shows that positive emotions are good for our health and affect medical outcomes.[1] Similarly, seeing a failed relationship as a lesson in intimacy, resilience, and humility will make us feel a whole lot better than shaping the story as one of self-sabotage and personal worthlessness.

In order to find the redemptive narrative, we first need to understand the transformational power of storytelling, be willing to wrestle with the scripts running our lives, and step out of our stories through the third-person voice so we can identify the places we get stuck. While it's true that we can't control everything that happens to us — in this way, we are not the sole authors of our stories — we can take charge of our story's narration, actively mining experiences for positive meaning. This power of interpretation is the heart of your personal power as coauthor of your story and the key to making meaningful improvements to your character.

An essential part of reframing your narrative with this particular lens is to redefine success. As you craft your story, I will ask you to recognize the subtle, often unrecognized personal victories that build character — such as facing a fear, changing an attitude, or kicking a bad habit. This is not necessarily how society traditionally measures success. When was the last time you bumped into a friend who announced, "Great news! Yesterday, I conquered my need for my boss's approval, and today I didn't scream at my son when he accidentally spilled milk all over the floor!"

These aren't the usual "happy endings" we crave. And that's okay. Sometimes, what we think will make us feel happy and successful — a six-figure income or a trophy spouse —

doesn't necessarily bring us the same level of inner peace or satisfaction that we experience when we break old problematic behavior patterns and change in positive ways we never imagined possible. For psychotherapists and writers, these kinds of changes mark meaningful progress in someone's lifelong development, whether that person is a client or an imagined character.

"Character development" is why I became a psychotherapist. It is also one of the reasons I go to the movies or pick up a book — I want to witness personal transformation and be transformed in the process. It is also the reason I wrote this book — to offer a new method for personal transformation by embracing one's destiny as an ever-evolving protagonist.

So shamelessly dive into the wonder of your own character, knowing that the treasures revealed will not only deeply enrich your life but also the stories of others whose lives you touch. As you weave seemingly fragmented pieces of your life into a coherent and meaningful new narrative, my hope and wish is that you will discover how character development is the heart of any story worth reading — and worth living.

What This Process Is and Is Not

This is not a book about writing your memoir. In fact, it's not about writing at all. Whether you can turn a nice phrase, or use punctuation properly, has no bearing on the nectar that can be extracted from this process.

Rather, this book is about deconstructing and reconstructing your personal narrative using a very specific type of architecture — the elements of a story. While there is no particular right or wrong way to do this, there is a best way.

For starters, I suggest you use this book to more deeply understand, work through, and of course positively reframe your experience of your life's current chapter, especially if you are feeling stuck in old, unhelpful storylines. I emphasize the *present* moment because now is the optimal time to change your story, but also, applying this framework to your whole life is an enormous undertaking. That said, at the end of the book, I invite you to do so if you wish.

However, I think you will reap the greatest benefit from the exercises if you try to write only a single "chapter" of your life, one that, like a typical book chapter, restricts itself to a discrete, limited stretch of time — typically several months to at most a year.

As you identify that period, you will reconstruct your story, element by element, eventually reassembling all these pieces into an empowering new narrative about where you are now and where you're heading.

How This Book Is Constructed

The book follows the classic story arc (as illustrated here and explained in chapter 1), which is designed to give you a sense of being walked through the natural progression of your story. Each step will provide you with a new piece of scaffolding for your story remodeling, with each element building on the one that preceded it. Here's how the process flows:

EXPOSITION: Chapters 1 through 7 introduce the basic concepts of this method and invite you to explore who you are as the hero or heroine of your own narrative. You will:

- learn how "the story lens on life" or "novel perspective" can help you reclaim and reframe your personal narrative;
- see how writing about yourself in the third-person narrative can free you from your inner critic, helping you to see your storyline through gentler, more compassionate eyes;
- discover what it means to be the hero or heroine of your own story;
- identify your character arc through a common author technique known as the "character sketch";
- look at the roles and scripts that get in the way of playing your character to the best of your ability;
- name and describe the current chapter of your life;
- look at how the ways in which you spin your story are working for and against you; and
- distinguish the objective outer story from the subjective internal story.

CONFLICT: Once you've gotten better acquainted with your story's protagonist, chapters 8 through 11 harness this knowledge to help you identify personal growth opportunities in the current chapter of your life. You will:

- discover how the conflict for your narrative is really a character development workout;
- identify the primary antagonist in the current chapter of your story;
- redefine your antagonist as a personal trainer, pushing you (the protagonist) to strengthen and tone underdeveloped emotional muscles;

- craft illuminating dialogues between you and your vulnerabilities and growing edges; and
- take stock of all the positive forces assisting you in rising to the challenges presented by your antagonist.

CLIMAX: After marshaling your collective strengths and resources, you're ready for the pinnacle of your story in chapter 12 where you will:

- envision your ideal climax and consider what you can do to make it happen;
- write a constructive dialogue with your antagonist; and
- give yourself the blessing you seek.

RESOLUTION: Having reached the climax, in chapters 12 and 13 you'll have a chance to find the redemptive, silver-lining narrative as you:

- reflect on what closure means to you;
- envision a resolution that leaves you feeling inspired.
- identify salient morals and themes that give your story meaning; and
- celebrate the obstacles you've overcome, what you have learned, and how much you've grown.

As you near the end of your journey with story, chapters 15 through 17 offer a wide-angle lens on your narrative, which you will put together into a new story. You will do the following:

- write an epilogue in which you begin to envision the next chapter of your story;

- reassemble all the story building blocks into a new and improved personal narrative about the current chapter of your life; and
- if you wish, use the story structure to explore your larger life narrative and begin to come to terms with unresolved chapters.

Some Advice Before You Start

As I say, I've found there is a "best" or most fruitful approach to writing your story in this context. As you begin, keep these things in mind:

Complete the Exercises in Order

As a recovering self-help junkie and habitual flouter of convention, I understand the temptation to skip around, completing perhaps only those exercises that speak to you in the moment. However, because this book is designed as a progressive series of exercises that follows the arc of a story, I strongly encourage you to complete the exercises in order. With each exercise, you will acquire tools and insights that will assist you in completing subsequent exercises.

That's not to say that you can't complete the exercises out of sequence and be successful. Certainly, depending on how long you take to complete this process, the circumstances of your "chapter" may shift, requiring adjustments and revisions. However, if you don't take too many breaks along the way, and if you define your chapter broadly enough, you should find that the basic elements — for example, the antagonist, the supporting characters, and the protagonist's growing edges — remain relevant. If you do happen to stop partway through and pick up the book again after a long lag (say, over a year), I would recommend going back to near the beginning, either to the character sketch in chapter 2 or the plot summary in chapter 6.

Once you get the hang of the method, however, feel free to use this process more than once, perhaps skipping around to your favorite exercises or to those that you think will help provide needed insight into a given situation.

Use the Same Notebook for All Exercises

I also recommend using one journal, or one computer or laptop, to complete the exercises. Some chapters refer to previous exercises, and you will want all your work at your fingertips. If you're like me, and you tend to use multiple notebooks, you may forget which one contains those inspired, middle-of-the-night epiphanies about your life purpose, and you may find yourself variously frustrated at different junctures. For example, chapter 7 asks you to identify the antagonist in the chapter 6 plot summary exercise, and you want to be able to turn to that plot summary immediately. Of course, you could write another summary, but consistency is preferred.

Write in the Third Person Unless Otherwise Directed

With a few noted exceptions (mainly for dialogues and at the very end), almost all the writing exercises are framed in the third-person voice. If you think, "Oh, I wasn't expecting that. That's not how I normally write, and I'm not even sure I'll like it," try it anyway. Whenever I announce in my workshops that we will be spending an afternoon writing in the third person, participants often give me strange, worried looks. But 9.5 times out of 10, they end up surprised by how much freer they feel to explore their stories from fresh angles and perspectives. Think of it this way: The first time you send a text message, typing with your thumbs seems counterintuitive, but eventually it becomes almost second nature. Similarly, writing in the third person may feel unnatural at first. But do it once or twice and you'll get the hang of it and really enjoy it.

Don't Worry about Writing Well

As I say, your masterpiece of living does not have to be, and isn't meant to be, a masterpiece of writing. While I encourage word play from time to time, crafting crisp, clean sentences is not the point of the exercises. In this case, writing is meant to serve as a tool for self-discovery, not self-torture or eventual publication. That said, several people have found that the third-person format and story arc structure is a useful springboard for writing their memoir. I'm happy if this process helps you in that way — more power to you — but once again, it's not the point.

If you find yourself obsessing about the right wording, or worrying about how things read or might sound to others, I invite you to stop, take a deep breath, and think about what your seven-year-old self would write. In my experience facilitating workshops, I've noticed that the written equivalent of stick-figure drawings may actually teach us more about ourselves than carefully crafted (and controlled) adult sentences. The goal is not writing well; the goal is self-discovery. The goal is to write powerfully and authentically.

Even though I have provided you with a solid framework from which to explore your story, creativity is not linear. If you get stuck, try using images and metaphors (mixed metaphors are fine; don't fuss over them) to help you move on.

When appropriate, you might answer questions in a list format instead of writing a narrative.

I also provide several writing examples to illustrate how to do the exercises. Students have told me they find the examples tremendously helpful, so please refer to them if you're unclear about instructions. I also use the *Wizard of Oz* and other pop culture references to illustrate how some of my concepts show up in recognizable stories.

Follow the Yellow Brick Road

How do you begin this journey of personal transformation? One step at a time, and knowing that the journey itself holds the answers that you seek. As Dorothy learns, there is no Great and Powerful Oz who can whisk you away in a magic balloon and deliver you effortlessly to a happy ending. Instead, like Glinda the Good Witch, I offer you tools that will help you step out of your story, reclaim the power of your own voice, and find your way home by exercising your innate ability to be the master of your own magnificent work in progress. I also invite you to step into your power as a storyteller and spin doctor, fortified with the conviction that personal transformation is both literally and figuratively at your fingertips. All you need is a pen (or a keyboard) and a sense of adventure. So put on your story glasses, shift your perspective, and enjoy the journey!

CHAPTER ONE

EMBRACING THE STORY LENS ON LIFE

Whether I shall turn out to be the hero of my own life, or whether that station will be held by anybody else, these pages must show.

— Charles Dickens, *David Copperfield*

Every life is an unfolding story, a dynamic, unique, purposeful, and potentially heroic story with bright spots, turning points, and abounding opportunities for personal growth and transformation. From the day we're born, we become the star and spin doctor of our own work in progress, with the power to tell our stories as triumphs, tragedies, or something in between. Our story has supporting characters who provide love and assistance and antagonists who cause us to realize the substance we're made of and what's really important. Like

stories, our lives are filled with suspense. Our personal decisions, both big and small, affect our storyline — the relationships we choose, how we spend our day, and how we nourish
ourselves physically, mentally, emotionally, and spiritually.

Yet few of us take time to explore the character we're playing. We don't stop to discover what our story is about, who's
writing our script, and how the challenges we face can help
us develop the insights and skills we need to move to the next
chapter.

Stuck in the same old story, many of us remain so entrenched in tales of victimization and martyrdom that we can
scarcely imagine an alternate, positive, or redemptive reading
of the text of our lives. Perhaps because we have been taught
to view life through one particular lens, we simply don't see
other, more inspiring versions of our tale that could liberate us.

Whether we realize it or not, we are constantly sifting
through various competing narratives to make sense of our
world for ourselves and others — whether it's describing our
day to a loved one, explaining why we didn't get promoted,
sharing our political perspective, or justifying why we spend a
fortune on organic produce. We may struggle with many con-
tradictory stories to explain our biggest decisions: why we got
divorced, or never had children, or changed careers, or never
pursued our dreams. Our perspective can change from day to
day, and even moment to moment, depending on our mood
and where exactly we are situated in the timeline of a problematic chapter. For example, the bitter tale we tell a month after
ending a failed romance is probably not the sentimental story
we will tell twenty years later after we are happily married to
someone else. And neither of these stories will be the same as
our former romantic partner's, even though it's the story of the
same relationship.

You can see this for yourself. Think of something funny, touching, interesting, or meaningful that has happened to you in the past few months. Now imagine telling this story to your spouse or your best friend. When you're done, imagine describing the same story to a parent or a boss. What about to a stranger in a café? What about five years from now, or twenty years? How might it be different?

While some details might remain the same, you might, depending on your audience, emphasize certain aspects of the story over others, or omit certain details that seem irrelevant, inappropriate, or too complicated to explain. As you tell it over and over, you might remember certain parts you had forgotten initially, or new insights might lead you to spin the story in a totally different direction. Over time, your values might change, and so you would revise your story accordingly, or hindsight might connect once-disparate episodes of your life.

Following a loss or a tragedy, many people engage in a prolonged period of story-wrestling in an attempt to make meaning of events that are hard to digest or that seem to defy explanation. Whether you consider yourself a heroic figure overcoming obstacles or a tragic victim of destiny often depends on how you choose to read the text of your life and the way that you tell your story. Take Milo's story, for instance.

Milo's Story: Superstar or Glorified Hack?

Milo, a thirty-one-year-old political reporter, had recently begun working at a fledgling online news magazine when an editor from another major newspaper invited him for coffee. He met the editor in her office, where she peppered him with questions about his new employer and complimented him on his increasingly visible body of work. On the way out, Milo shared an elevator with his hero and mentor, who had helped him break into the industry ten years earlier. Milo, who often second-guessed his abilities, felt reassured. This seemed like a sign that he was on a right path.

However, following the meeting, Milo attended a press conference with a local politician, who scoffed at one of his questions. Suddenly, all the good feelings from the morning evaporated, and he felt like a glorified hack.

Later that evening during our psychotherapy session together, Milo recounted the chain of events. He said he regretted his choice of questions at the press conference; they were an embarrassing error. Consequently, he wondered if the positive meaning he had read into the morning meeting at the daily newspaper had been "a lie."

As a psychotherapist with a background in journalism, I gave the matter some thought and framed my answer as a metaphor: "It's like writing an inspirational chapter of a story and erasing it because of a typo."

Reclaiming and Reframing Your Personal Narrative

Milo's story raises an important question. If there are a variety of ways to view our story, how do we choose the best version of our narrative so that the telling leaves us feeling inspired and hopeful? How do we find the redemptive storyline without whitewashing over unpleasant circumstances, repressing feelings, or discounting important life lessons?

For starters, you need a framework for understanding your story so you can explore what's positive, redemptive, and possibly inspirational about it. Ideally, this framework would be something simple and relatively familiar that would help you take charge of the narration of your story adventure. Additionally, it would place importance on character development, reframing any disappointments or losses as stepping-stones to a more open-hearted or broad-minded experience of life and a richer understanding of yourself. It would measure your worth — not based on the number of zeros in your salary, on your job title, or on your marital status — but rather, on the extent to which you, in the starring role, could grow in compassion, wisdom, depth, and responsibility regardless of circumstances. Finally, when you stepped outside your story to look at the full picture of your life, you would discover that no matter what was happening in your plotline, you held the power to be cocreator of your story by reframing how you perceived and shared it.

Next, you need a new lens on life, one that elevates your perspective, frees your imagination, and overrides your inner critic. This new and improved prescription, so to speak, would help you view "the same old story" from new vistas and through kinder, more empathetic eyes.

Thankfully, you don't have to reinvent the wheel — both the lens and the frames already exist. And you're probably familiar with both of them — it just never occurred to apply these lessons to your own life. The lens I'm referring to is the third-person voice and the framework, the elements of a story. Not what you were expecting? Let me explain.

Putting On Your Story Glasses

Perhaps you recall learning the elements of a story in school. I can still picture my grade-school teacher drawing the curve on the chalkboard as she explained that every story has a hero who is working toward a goal or a dream, an antagonist who gets in the way, and a conflict between two forces that builds to a climax and leads to a resolution, transforming the protagonist for better or worse.

Even if you slept through this particular class, the format should seem familiar. For all of us, the narrative arc is imprinted into our developing brains from the moment we hear our first bedtime story and watch our first cartoon on television, following a favorite character through some madcap or fearsome adventure while hoping for a happy outcome. We become conditioned to this simple story arc, which emerges whenever we, ourselves, tell a story. We might tell slightly different versions of the same story — whether we are speaking to our friends, our shrink, or the passenger sitting next to us on an overseas flight. But whether we are explaining how we overcame shyness to become a newscaster, or found love again after a horrible divorce, we typically cast ourselves as a protagonist who has overcome obstacles and grown through challenges.

These plot elements are like the architecture of a story. Just as architects need to know structural design, we need to understand the specific ways that each of these elements directs and supports our growth as an ever-evolving protagonist so that we can reconstruct a strong and powerful new narrative from the raw materials of our one precious life.

Chances are you've had a graduation, a wedding, or maybe even a kid or two since your last English class. If you need to get acquainted, or reacquainted, with the elements of storytelling, don't worry; the next chapter will teach you all about them. The diagram below gives you some of the key elements you'll be working with. For now, keep these general descriptions in mind:

EXPOSITION: Introduces characters, setting, and background information, usually at the beginning of a story.

PROTAGONIST: The main character of the story. In most storylines, the protagonist is trying to accomplish something, win something, find something, or defeat something.[2]

SETTING: The time and place where a story is situated.

PLOT: The sequence of events that make up a story. This includes the outer story, or what actually happened, and the inner story, or how the character experienced it.

ANTAGONIST: Usually the protagonist's nemesis. The antagonist might be a person (boss, parent, ex-spouse) or an obstacle that must be overcome or reconciled with (prejudice, poverty, aging, addiction).

CONFLICT: The central problem in a story, usually between the protagonist and antagonist. Stories can have multiple conflicts (and multiple antagonists), but one typically plays itself out through rising action that leads to the story's climax.

CLIMAX: The turning point of the story, when suspense over how the conflict will be resolved reaches its peak.

FALLING ACTION: The events that transpire following the climax as the story winds down, approaching resolution.

RESOLUTION: The conclusion of the conflict, when stock is taken and the story ends.

MORAL OR THEME: The underlying message of a story.

EPILOGUE: After the resolution of the conflict, a description of following events that often ties up loose ends.

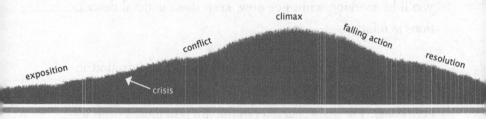

Applying the Novel Perspective

When you superimpose this "novel perspective" onto the story of your life, you change the way you value and find meaning in experiences.

After all, the human mind is wired to search for patterns, to organize what it notices in its environment into a digestible coherent form. This is how we extract meaning from what could seem like random events. Our minds can be like messy desks, and we may struggle to process all the information we absorb — to know which fragments are worth holding on to and how to properly file them so that the categories make intuitive sense and help us flourish. While there are as many organizing systems as there are frameworks for understanding the world, few are as familiar or ingrained as the story structure. The story is "a natural package for many different kinds of information," explains Dr. Daniel P. McAdams, a professor of psychology at Northwestern University and the director of the Foley Center for the Study of Lives. "When we comprehend our actions over time, we see what we do in terms of a story. We see obstacles confronted, and intentions realized and frustrated over time. As we move forward from yesterday to tomorrow, we move through tensions building to climaxes, climaxes giving way to denouements, and tensions building again as we continue to move and change. Human time is a storied affair."[3]

We might even say that suffering can sometimes partly be due to a storytelling deficit, a failure to find a good filing system that organizes the details of one's life into a meaningful cause-and-effect narrative, which results in an incoherent or distorted story.

For example, let's say you're unemployed, and you tell yourself the story that this is just another crappy situation that defines your very difficult life. You ask yourself, "Why does this always happen to me?" Then you finally land a job interview. What happens? This negative story may lead you to wonder, "What's the point?" And this negative vibe may lead you to botch the job interview, which causes more suffering and only confirms your negative story.

However, what if you saw the antagonist (in this case, unemployment) of the current chapter in your life (a chapter you might entitle "A Thousand Resumes") as the necessary force that is pushing you to resolve your main conflict: perhaps that you are in fact ambivalent about this career path or that you tend to get easily discouraged. In a way, this antagonist is like a personal trainer, and this conflict is the force challenging you to develop your confidence or to become clear about your career direction. Suddenly, as you exercise control over how you view your situation, the time between jobs becomes an invitation to work on yourself and build your muscles. Through this lens, you might say to yourself, "If I were reading this chapter in a book about the story of my life, I might appreciate that unemployment is nudging me — the protagonist — to get more organized and keep persevering in the face of adversity. I can choose to embrace that challenge, and forge ahead, or drain myself of valuable energy by sinking into discouragement."

Cast in this light, the power of interpretation via the story lens on life offers a powerful elixir for heartbreaks, disappointments, and existential angst.

Jill's Story: Defining Happily Ever After

Take Jill's story. From the time Jill met Tom in her senior year of college, they were practically inseparable. The native New Englanders seemed like the perfect match — they were both politically active and shared many interests, including the outdoors, vegan cooking, science fiction, and a dream of living out west. Following graduation, they moved to San Francisco, where they landed decent entry-level jobs in their respective fields. Three years later, as their friends began getting engaged, Jill broached the subject of marriage and children with Tom. While Tom seemed receptive to marriage, he told Jill that he didn't want to have children.

Jill, who always dreamed of being a mother, was devastated. She had sensed a certain apprehension from Tom whenever she mentioned children, but she had never pushed him, partly because she feared confirming her suspicions. They tried counseling, but Tom, who had been somewhat neglected as a child and had strong political views about global overpopulation, was adamant about his position.

Jill was in crisis and confused. Her parents and friends were pressuring her to break up with him and move on. She had never lived entirely on her own, and the thought of being alone, without Tom, so far from her close-knit family, scared her. Should she stay with Tom, the man she loved and considered her soul mate, and give up her lifelong dream of having children?

How can embracing the story lens on life help Jill? Well, it won't prevent her from experiencing sadness, anger, guilt, confusion, and fear — or all the natural, understandable human emotions that arise during difficult times. Nor should it. From a psychological perspective, feeling our feelings is an important part of emotional maturation, as well as a prerequisite for intimacy.

Yet thoroughly considering each of the story elements in her life's current chapter can help her figure out the best way to move forward. All the story elements — San Francisco (the setting), their childhood dreams and experiences (exposition), the plot (the love story), and the conflict (the disagreement about having children) — are interacting with one another to create a crisis that is pushing for a resolution. In the world of stories, that's a good thing. The conflict between the protagonist (Jill) and the antagonist (Tom) has led to tension that must be resolved to move Jill's story forward. To move forward, Jill is compelled to look within and make courageous choices informed by a deeper understanding of her needs and values.

Imagining her life in the third person can help give Jill the necessary critical distance to meet and resolve this dilemma, which is really a test of her courage, faith, and inner truth. Is this conflict an opportunity to push past her fear of being alone? Or is it about accepting that her life's priorities have changed — that her love for Tom and her life with him is now more significant than her childhood vision of having children? Either way, Jill has taken charge of her story, so that she will experience her choice as life-affirming, transformational, and ultimately in her best interest.

In this way, looking through the story lens can help reframe difficult life events without creating unnecessary drama. Obviously, if you lost your job, caught your husband cheating, or you lost your job on the day you caught your husband cheating, the point isn't to say, "At least I have a compelling story to tell. My soon-to-be-ex-husband sure makes a vivid character!" But if we can place our stories in a recognizable context, understanding that all the story elements are conspiring toward our ultimate benefit, we have a better chance of making wise decisions and finding the meaningful silver-lining narrative in whatever plot twists life throws at us.

CHAPTER TWO

SHIFTING YOUR PERSPECTIVE

Imagine walking into a neighborhood bookstore and discovering a novel with a familiar picture on the cover. Flipping through the pages, you are struck by the eerie sense that you've read this before. As you recognize characters and scenes, wincing at some and smiling at others, you realize this is the story of your life. If this happened, would you feel love and compassion for the main character, or would you scrutinize the character's every word and action?

According to the latest research, you are more likely to view your life favorably at a distance than up close. Psychological studies suggest that reflecting on your life, both in the past and present, as a third-person observer can help you see yourself and the things you've overcome through fresher and more compassionate eyes.

That's why once you've put on your story glasses, you need to change your prescription...to the third-person narrative. Third-person narration is one of three types of literary points of view: First-person narrative uses the pronoun "I" and is used when the narrator tells his or her own story. Second-person narrative uses the pronoun "you" and is used when the narrator speaks directly to the reader, like I am speaking to you right now. Third-person narrative uses the pronouns "he," "she," and "they," and it is used when the narrator describes someone else's story, often from a neutral or all-knowing perspective. For this reason, it is sometimes referred to as the omniscient narrator. Researchers conclude that the psychologically distant vantage point of the third-person perspective enables people to reconstruct an understanding of their experiences and gain new insights without feeling emotionally overwhelmed. (See the sidebar "What Research Says about the Third-Person Narrative," below.)

What Research Says about the Third-Person Narrative

Here are some recent studies that confirm how helpful a third-person perspective can be when viewing our own emotions and life.

- Stanford University psychologists studying emotion regulation asked a group of women who were hooked up to a machine measuring heart rate, pulse, and perspiration to recall a scene that made them angry. At first, the women's ruminations sent their nervous systems into overdrive. Then the women were asked to visualize the incident as a neutral observer, or to assume the perspective of another person, and their bodies became calmer and their anger diminished.[4]

- University of California and University of Michigan researchers used a psychologically distancing vantage point when asking participants to reflect on negative memories. Not only did participants report less emotional pain, less rumination, improved problem solving, and greater life satisfaction, they also gained new insights into those memories without feeling as emotionally overwhelmed.[5]

- In an Ohio State University study, students who recalled humiliating moments in high school in the third-person narrative were more likely to describe themselves as having overcome obstacles than those who recalled similarly embarrassing moments from a first-person perspective. Participants in this group often portrayed themselves as victims. The study concluded that feeling like you've changed gives the confidence and momentum to act in ways that support a perceived new and improved self.[6]

- In a Columbia University study, students were asked to describe recently upsetting thoughts or feelings, and these bad memories were recalled with less hostility by those using the third-person perspective.[7]

- A University of Michigan study was done through the use of a six-day worry log. Results showed people writing in the third person reported higher life satisfaction. Researchers concluded that "self-distancing...provides a valuable framework to help people reframe stressful events in adaptive ways."[8]

This makes sense when we consider how much our identity is deeply intertwined with our first-person narrative — the big "I," otherwise known as the ego. A good, healthy "I" is necessary for establishing relationships, launching enterprises, and navigating life's ups and downs. If we didn't have a healthy sense of "I," we might find it difficult to distinguish our thoughts and feelings from those of the people around us, so that we mostly mimicked or reflected our parents, peers, and society while losing our sense of individuality and autonomy. For these reasons, our "I" perspective is very important to us, and it can be hard to see past it.

I, I, I: The Negating Narrators

And yet, sometimes we invest so much in our "I" that this perspective gets in the way of adopting a helpful bird's eye view of our story. The third-person perspective can be easily obstructed by our censoring ego and our inner critic, or what I like to describe as our two "negating narrators."

The first type of negating narrator, and the least harmful, is like a worried helicopter parent who keeps you from straying too far outside your comfort zone. The motivation of the "censoring ego" is to keep you safe, free from self-discoveries that can potentially overwhelm you by contradicting your preconceived self-image. One of the challenges of this narrator is that it often underestimates the strength and bandwidth of your character.

The other type of negating narrator, the inner critic, is like a parent for whom nothing is ever good enough. When this negating narrator takes charge, self-exploration can easily degenerate into criticism. It reads your story through the lens of judgment,

pointing out your mistakes and shortcomings. Its motivation is
to keep you small, and it often leaves you feeling deflated.

Because they're protecting our ego, negating narrators
tend to show up when we write or think about ourselves in the
first-person voice. When we declare "I am this" or "I think
that," our negating narrators can guide and cling to the descrip-
tors that follow. For example, if we say "I am a successful stock-
broker" or "I am a stay-at-home mother," we may be misled
into believing that is all we are while discounting other valuable
parts of our personality. Such distorted thinking may trigger
an identity crisis if that label is challenged by external circumstances, like the market crashing or children leaving the nest.

The genius of writing in the third person is that it sneaks us
past our negating narrators, who think that we are describing
someone else's life. After all, you're not writing about yourself
(wink, wink), you're describing the character of your first, second, or third novel!

Writing about yourself in the third person creates an opening to be more curious about the direction of your own unfolding story. For example, instead of fearing the unknown, you
might wonder what this protagonist will do next — will she
accept the marriage proposal or join the Peace Corps and go to
Africa? Such a viewpoint can increase your sense of satisfaction and compassion toward yourself, or alternatively, it can
serve as a wake-up call if the character you are playing doesn't
fit the picture of who you imagine yourself to be.

This latter point is comically depicted in the fantasy film
Stranger than Fiction, in which Harold Crick, a robotic IRS
agent played by Will Ferrell, begins to question his mundane
existence when he hears a mysterious voice narrating his life
and foreshadowing his untimely death. The narrator in his head

casts him in the role of a bureaucratic automaton whose tragic demise is a justifiable response to his passionless, unexamined life. When he discovers that he is not the master of his own destiny, but rather a fictional character dreamed up by an eccentric British author named Karen Eifel, Crick tracks down his creator and, by taking a more active role in his life, convinces her to rewrite the ending of his story. Not only does Crick survive the bus accident that is supposed to kill him, he gets the girl, saves a child, and emerges from the whole experience with a richer, more vibrant, and deliciously textured perspective on the meaning of life.

While both strange and fictional, Crick's journey is a wonderful illustration of the exciting possibilities that await us when we reclaim the coauthorship rights of our personal narratives. From the perch of the third-person narrative, we can step out of our stories, check out the landscape, and determine whether to stay on the road we're taking or reroute. From there, who knows what we'll discover?

First Person vs. Third Person Warm-up

Now, see for yourself the difference between writing in the first and third person in this simple warm-up exercise. In it, you can get a sense of what it feels like when you switch narrative perspectives.

First, write a paragraph in the first-person voice describing a time in the recent past when you did something that you really didn't want to do, but you did it because you knew it was in your best interest. This might be a difficult conversation with a friend or your boss, or perhaps it was a chore for a loved one. Be sure to describe your feelings before and after the event. For example:

I didn't want to look at it — the stack of papers on my desk, with all kinds of evidence of how I had been negligent in attending to my taxes the past year and of all the income I had hoped to but didn't make. I had fooled myself into thinking that I had done okay financially, managed to cover my rent, pay my bills, fill my refrigerator, buy some new clothes, and even have a few short vacations. But the truth lay in that pile. As I began to dig through it, I felt a surge of anxiety in my chest and an old, familiar feeling — shame. How had I managed to survive all these years while being so financially incompetent? People thought I was so together. If only they knew.

Next, write a new paragraph describing the *same* dreaded chore in the third person. For example:

She wasn't particularly organized. She had other strengths — creativity, intelligence, a good sense of humor — but keeping on top of her finances, well, that left much to be desired. At least she knew the documents that needed to be saved, even if she stuck them in folders and refused to look at them until she had absolutely no other option. But April 15 came around every year, forcing her to face the spreadsheets. She could delude herself into thinking that she had done okay financially, but the numbers never lied. She'd see how much she made and what she owed, and the penalties she'd incurred from forgetting to pay her estimated taxes. It was her secret shame. Yet she took some comfort in knowing she was far from the only one. And her situation wasn't so bad. Some people didn't pay taxes for years, like her friend's ex-husband — what a disaster! As

far as the nitty-gritty number crunching was concerned,
that's what accountants were for, right? Her accountant
would figure it all out and keep her out of the government
doghouse.

When you're done, take a few minutes to reflect on what
it felt like to write in the third person. Some students have
described having more positive feelings toward their third-
person self than they normally do toward themselves when
they write in the first person. If not, be patient. Writing in the
third person is a bit like asking righties to use their left hand.
I encourage you to get uncomfortable, experimenting outside
your comfort zone, and see what unfolds. Next, we'll start the
process itself in the place where most stories begin, getting to
know the star of your story, the protagonist otherwise known
as you!

CHAPTER THREE

GETTING TO KNOW
THE STAR OF YOUR STORY

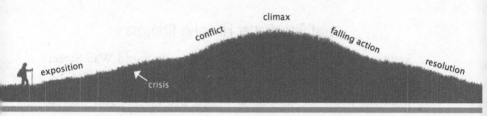

Men go abroad to wonder at the heights of mountains, at the huge waves of the sea, at the long courses of the rivers, at the vast compass of the ocean, at the circular motions of the stars, and they pass by themselves without wondering.

— St. Augustine of Hippo, *Confessions*

Exposition: The beginning of a story in which the main character is introduced to the reader. Situating the story in a time and place, the exposition presents important descriptive information that is needed to fully understand the protagonist.

Now that you've put on your story glasses and changed your perspective to the third person, it's time to get better acquainted with the star of your story — you. Every human story is also a journey of transformation. We start out in one place, with a particular outlook, and end up in another. Yet rarely do we explore who we are as evolving characters with the same gusto and curiosity that we reserve for foreign travel — that is, until something forces us to take a closer look at the person behind the passport. Take Seymour's story, for instance.

Lost Globetrotter Finds His Compass

Seymour was a single, white, thirty-nine-year-old Wall Street financial professional who "loved to travel" — at least, that's what he wrote in his online dating profile. He had toured through Australia, trekked up Machu Picchu, and visited several beach resorts in four continents. Yet Seymour was lonely, and he was dissatisfied with his career. Although he often sought out classically beautiful women, he usually got bored a few months into the relationship. At work, he felt restless and distracted. When he wasn't stressed, he entertained himself by composing songs in his head, though his masterpieces never saw daylight.

The trouble was, while Seymour had seen many parts of the world, he had barely explored the recesses of his own heart. An only child, Seymour had grown up somewhat emotionally neglected. His kindly but stoic father, who had worked in construction, had died of a heart attack when Seymour was only eleven. His mother, a nurse, had often worked overtime to put food on the table and send her son to college, and she had suffered periodic bouts of depression that sometimes left her bedridden. With little personal attention and guidance, Seymour turned to television and peers for clues about how to find happiness, but the proffered solutions — making money and womanizing — left him feeling empty.

When he thought of himself as the protagonist of his own story, Seymour recognized where this particular character arc would end if he didn't change: with the character becoming a lonely, rich, and unhappy man. Seymour also worried about dying young, like his father. Instead, he wanted more inspiring work that left him with the same sense of enthusiasm he felt returning from his travels. The idea arose of starting an international importing business using some of his overseas contacts. He also wanted to learn how to play the guitar. With the right woman, he could build a family of his own. But to do all this, he first needed to take charge of his story, get to the bottom of his emotional blocks, and get better acquainted with his true self. His happiness and health were at stake.

What's Your Character Arc?

While you can't predict your future, you can take charge of the direction of your character arc if you're willing to explore your protagonist's terrain with the same sense of adventure and awe you would bring to a trek through the Himalayas.

Every protagonist has a character arc, a particular way he or she matures and develops in response to the shifting tides of the story. This area of growth is the threshold between the hero's present self and his or her aspirational self; some call this a person's "growing edge," a term I like and use in this book. At the outset of every narrative, the protagonist possesses certain viewpoints and capabilities that have gotten the character by until now. Inevitably, situations arise that challenge these perspectives or demand other skills the hero doesn't yet possess, thus creating the main conflict of the narrative. After all, if the character already possessed the necessary skills or a broader perspective, there would be no challenge and no conflict in the story. Ultimately, the protagonist faces an opportunity to change in some way. The degree to which the protagonist embraces this challenge, and his or her growing edge, or tries to avoid the challenge determines who he or she becomes, for better or for worse.

Similarly, you are an ever-evolving protagonist on a journey of self-discovery with choices to make about how to respond to the stuff that happens in your life. As an ever-evolving protagonist, not only do you possess the power to adapt to plot twists, but you can view these unexpected difficulties as opportunities for personal growth and transformation. In fact, you can coauthor your own story by regarding every person and situation that shows up in your narrative as an invitation to further hone a different aspect of your character, or one of your growing edges.

That, of course, includes antagonists — the so-called villains and foils that make life challenging — as well as supporting characters and any life events, welcome and unwelcome. After all, just because your life is a story doesn't mean it's supposed to be a fairy tale. In fact, even fairy tales aren't joy rides. If you study them carefully, you'll notice that serious difficulties always beset the main characters before they get to their happy ending. Cinderella may meet her prince and become transformed, but she has to sweep a whole bunch of chimneys, and endure much humiliation, before she gets there. Jack has to outrun a homicidally hungry giant to capture his treasure in the sky. We not only expect that the main characters of stories will be challenged in some essential way, but we anticipate it.

In stories, the status quo is not just boring, it's unacceptable. Whether we consciously recognize it or not, could it be that deep down we understand that something needs to happen to the main character for his or her own good or, dare I say, growth? If so, then why is it that it's so easy to lose this perspective when it comes to telling the story of our own life, when our own status quo is shaken? As the protagonist of our own heroic narrative, doesn't it seem silly not to recognize that the things that happen to us are what offer opportunities to actualize our potential, calling forth perhaps dormant aspects of our personality that we need to resolve the situation?

Life constantly presents us with challenges. Should we choose to meet them, these keep us growing and evolving from chapter to chapter. Sure, you may not have a wicked witch chasing you like Dorothy in *The Wizard of Oz*, but chances are you've had to contend with being lost, dealing with difficult people, and accepting that the authority figures you counted on did not deserve your trust.

Unlike some of the heroes from fairy tales and popular fiction, however, you don't necessarily need to vanquish your nemesis — you simply need to explore who you are as an evolving character and understand your narrative.

Embracing Your Inner Hero or Heroine

Human beings are natural-born storytellers. In his book *The Stories We Live By*, psychologist Dan McAdams, director of the Foley Center for the Study of Lives, holds that, whether or not we realize it, every individual "comes to know who he or she is by creating a heroic story of the self."[9] These personal myths help us weave together disparate threads from the past, present, and anticipated future into a coherent and meaningful narrative that captures who we are and hope to become. As McAdams explains:

> If you want to know me, then you must know my story, for my story defines who I am. And if I want to know myself,... then I too must come to know my story.... It is the story I continue to revise, and tell to myself (and sometimes to others) as I go on living.... This is not the stuff of delusion or self-deception. We are not telling ourselves lies. Rather, through our personal myths, each of us discovers what is true and what is meaningful in life. [10]

Occasionally, however, people balk when I invite them to embrace their inner hero. They wonder if such concentrated focus on their own story is self-indulgent navel-gazing or even narcissistic. If you have similar reservations, the following distinction will hopefully alleviate any concerns.

One primary difference between self-discovery and contemplating one's belly button is intention. Navel-gazing is typically an end in itself; it describes when we become preoccupied with our own emotions, thoughts, and internal world at the expense of relating to others. Self-discovery, however, is about self-awareness; we explore our thoughts, feelings, preferences, talents, and vulnerabilities so that we might see ourselves as others do and improve our ability to relate with others and succeed in the world. The aim of this type of introspection is to enhance our capacity for love, compassion, understanding, and self-reflection. Self-discovery presumes that intimate knowledge of oneself precedes the ability to know and be intimate with others. The more we understand who we are, what makes us tick, the more we can share our gifts with other people and society.

Second, your story matters. Every person's story matters. We are moved and affected by all the stories around us. When we marvel at public figures, athletes, and individuals who overcome tremendous odds to accomplish great feats, we regard their life stories as transformative and important. Their stories inspire everyone to make similar difficult, heroic, or compassionate choices in their own ways. Consider great humanitarians like Nelson Mandela and Mahatma Gandhi. They spent considerable time in self-reflection, developing self-awareness, and valuing the importance of their own narratives — not to congratulate themselves but in order to serve causes larger than themselves.

In this regard, when we think of ourselves as the protagonist in our own story, and cultivate that story, it is not self-absorption but our birthright. Each of us needs to know our own story because it helps us define and understand who we are in the world and what it means to be human. The great and wonderful irony, of course, is that the more intimate we become with our story, the more we realize that everyone has their own equally valid and important narrative, of which they too are the central character.

Creating a Character Sketch

Once you've given yourself permission to embark on a journey of self-discovery, where do you start? Obviously, with the hero of your story (you).

When novelists first imagine and start to develop the main characters for their stories, they use a writing technique known as a character sketch. As you take hold of the authorship reins of your own narrative, I invite you to travel this time-tested path. In many ways, a character sketch is like taking the scenic route to your eventual story, one that leads you through new landscapes toward broader vistas. Only in this case, you are going to assume the role of both author *and* protagonist, using this proven storytelling device to get a richer understanding of your main character.

A character sketch is a technique that helps authors flesh out the personalities and interior world of the protagonist before embarking on a novel. It involves answering a series of imaginative questions that paint a holographic picture of how the protagonist might evolve over the course of the plotline. The character sketch presumes that the protagonist is the soul of every narrative and the engine that runs the story. By using this device to penetrate the hearts and minds of the protagonists they create, authors can help ensure that their heroes remain true to character, so to speak, in the actions they take and the choices they make.

So, too, you are the engine of your personal narrative. The more you understand about who you are, what you're made of, and what's driving you, the better equipped you'll be to navigate the twists in your plotline, steer your life narrative in a positive new direction, and avoid veering off course.

The character sketch is a perfect first step toward rewriting your story because it offers a well-groomed trailhead into our protagonist's journey with questions that can dependably lead you in constructive directions. Toward this end, the character sketch will become the basis for your story's exposition, the first building block of your reconstructed narrative. As the first element in the story arc, the exposition sets the stage for the plot, presenting important descriptive and background information that gives the reader a window into the protagonist's personality. This is important because the more you understand who you are as an ever-evolving protagonist, the more you can see where your story is heading and how you want to direct it.

Similarly, writing a character sketch will help you develop a richer appreciation for yourself as a character, laying a solid foundation for deeper explorations in your unfolding storyline later in this book. After all, personal transformation begins with self-awareness. You need to have a good grasp of the raw materials you're working with — your strengths, needs, desires, quirks, habits, and even your shortcomings — before you can shape your life into a work of art that reflects your purest and most imaginative vision.

Celebrated author and writing guru Anne Lamott describes the character sketch process as exploring the protagonist's "emotional acreage." In her bestselling book, *Bird by Bird: Some Instructions on Writing and Life*, Lamott explains that "each of your characters has an emotional acre that they tend, or don't tend, in certain specific ways. One of the things you want to discover as you start out is what each person's acre looks like. What is the person growing, and what sort of shape is the land in? ... The point is that you need to find out as much as possible about the interior life of the people you are working with."[11]

As you might imagine, each novelist has a slightly different approach. If you Google "character development questions," you'll find dozens of sites with hundreds of possible questions in varying levels of detail. They include basic demographic questions — how old, what ethnicity, where do they live, what type of education — as well as questions that probe their psychology and personality quirks: "What are the protagonist's fears, fantasies, and childhood wounds?" "What is the character's favorite breakfast, rock band, and footwear?" However, the four most comprehensive and essential questions are the following:

1. Who is the protagonist?
2. What does the protagonist want?
3. What is getting in the way?
4. What's at stake?

Of course, these lines of inquiry assume greater significance when the character you're exploring is you. If answering these questions about yourself feels a little scary, that's okay. It's natural to be emotionally invested in our own narratives. Thankfully, you have a new tool, writing in the third-person voice, which can free you up to explore your story with greater freedom and abandon.

Let's take a closer look at each of these questions.

1. Who Is the Protagonist?

The first thing I do when a new client walks into my therapy office is ask them for a personal history. I don't start this way simply because it's standard protocol. I ask because nothing happens in a vacuum. For every story, there is always a backstory. And in order to help people transform their narrative, I need to get a good read on who they are and how they came to be.

Human beings are dynamic and multidimensional. We are affected by forces inside us and around us. Not only are we products of our biology (of nature), we are also affected by our environment (by nurture). Family, culture, ethnicity, class, religion, and the generation we're born into, as well as the particular landscape of our childhood wounds, are just some of the forces that shape our character, influencing how we cope with stress, what secrets we keep, what makes us feel most alive, and what we fantasize about. Some forces are subtler than others, but everything becomes intertwined in who we are: the television shows we grew up watching, the kids who bullied us, the opportunities we had or missed because of our families' economic situation, and so on.

These forces continue to shape us throughout our lifetime, and the older we get, the more we discover our own particular interests, tastes, pace, and preferential ways of moving through life. Every individual, after all, is unique. No two people walk the planet in the same manner, on the same trajectory, leaving the same set of footprints — not even conjoined twins. Some schools of psychology go so far as to assert that self-articulation is the primary purpose of life. Psychologist Carl Jung, for example, maintained that a person's ability to find meaning and purpose in life is largely dependent on the degree to which he or she is able to individuate, or how we define ourselves on our own terms and come into our own.

Protagonist Exercise #1

Let's begin your character profile! On a clean piece of paper, choose at least five questions from the lists below, including at least two backstory questions. *Using the third-person voice,* weave them into a short descriptive narrative similar to what you'd read in a Cliff Notes version, on a book flap, or in a Playbill. If it feels daunting to write as if telling a story, you can simply answer each question individually in an explanatory fashion. But try stepping out of your story comfort zone. Either way, answering questions in the third person should make creating the profile easier.

Backstory Questions

- What are the basic facts about the protagonist, such as age, gender, marital status, place of residence, and so on?
- What was his or her childhood like?
- What is one strong memory that has stuck with your character from childhood? Why is it so powerful and lasting?[12]
- What are some of his or her proudest moments up until now?
- What are some wounds he or she has healed?
- What wounds still need some attention?

Who Is the Protagonist Today?

- How does the protagonist spend most of his or her free time?
- How does the protagonist self-identify — ethnically, spiritually, culturally, and religiously? What do these identities mean to the person?
- When does the protagonist feel most alive?
- How does he or she cope with stress?
- What are some secrets?
- What are some fantasies?
- What are some personality quirks?
- Imagine that your character is doing intense spring cleaning. What is easy to throw out? What is difficult to part with? Why?[13]

2. What Does the Protagonist Want?

At first glance, this seems like a fairly straightforward question. But actually, there are many possible responses. Human beings are virtual wanting machines, desiring many things immediately and at the same time. Such greedy seeking can scatter our energies, keeping us from choosing a goal with a clearly defined path.

That's why it helps to identify the protagonist's primary desire, his or her most basic aspiration and dream. Perhaps you, as the hero of your story, want a happy marriage, a six-figure salary, or for your children to get accepted into good colleges. Perhaps you want a better relationship with your parents, more (or less) responsibility in your job, or to join the Peace Corps.

You may feel comfortable telling the world what you want, or perhaps you keep secret the things you desire most, or only tell your closest family and friends. Perhaps you are a mid-level manager at a bank but secretly want to act on Broadway. Secret wishes tell us a lot about a protagonist; for example, they suggest whether he or she follows societal expectations or the stirrings of the heart.

As you ask this question, take a deeper look into your protagonist's motivations. Why does the protagonist want what he or she wants? In other words, ask, "What makes my protagonist tick?" Everyone has a longing that motivates their actions and drives their story forward. This thirst or hunger pushes them to overcome obstacles. Dorothy Gale seeks home; Harry Potter, to defend the good against the forces of evil.

In real life, both visible and invisible forces, called drives, push us to strive toward our goals. According to various schools of psychology, these drives are shaped in childhood mostly by our parents or caregivers, depending on which of our needs were satisfied and which not. People who never felt emotion-ally safe, for example, may be driven to find security through relationships, a community, or perhaps a religion that offers clear guidelines for living. Those who may not have felt seen or understood may be driven to express themselves through art, literature, dance, acting, and other forms of self-expression. Others who never felt good, important, or valuable enough may be driven to achieve a sense of mastery, to make them-selves indispensable, or to be financially successful. Other examples of drives include the desire to feel protected, peace-ful, competent, and optimistic.

Understanding what drives the protagonist of your story is important because it shows what he or she values, whether it's relationships, money, freedom, peace, authenticity, justice, or something else. It's also worth noting that what a character wants isn't necessarily what he or she needs. For example, we may want to win the lottery, but what we need for our own per-sonal evolution is to learn the value of hard work.

Since our motivations may not always be clear to us, taking a moment to ask yourself what the protagonist wants not only gives your story a sense of direction but sheds light on what you care about. After all, if we don't know what we want, we'll never figure out how to get it.

Protagonist Exercise #2

To understand your character's motivations, answer these ques-tions in the third-person voice.

- At this moment in time, what does the protagonist want?
- If you asked about his or her greatest dream, what would your character tell you?[14]

- What's a secret dream that he or she wouldn't tell you about?
- What may be driving this desire? Is it the need for unconditional love, security, a sense of power? Or is it a desire to be useful, or something else?
- What does he or she really need? Does this differ from what the protagonist wants, and if so, how?

3. What Is Getting in the Way?

Oftentimes, we want something, but we can't quite figure out how to get it. Because we live in a Western, materialistic society, many people think of obstacles in terms of people and things, or tangible obstacles. Perhaps we believe that money or physical beauty are standing in the way of fulfilling our dreams. Or we think that if only we had the right boss, or a more supportive spouse, or lived in a city, we'd finally be successful and happy.

These things can be obstacles, but sometimes we also get in our own way. Fear, regret, anger, resentment, and other unpleasant emotions may present formidable emotional obstacles that prevent us from moving forward; they can create distractions and lead to self-sabotage. For example, we might want to be in a romantic relationship, but we find we constantly pursue people who aren't available or don't want us. We may want to quit our jobs or change careers, but we might be too scared of failure to risk leaving. Oftentimes, we may get stuck because we fear change, or we fear being emotionally vulnerable because our hearts have been broken before. Holding onto resentments, lacking faith in ourselves — many things can keep us from pursuing our dreams.

Because it's hard to push past something that you don't see clearly, the mere act of reflecting on what is blocking your protagonist's path can help you consider the challenges you face from a different perspective. This theme will be further explored in chapter 8 on the role of the antagonist in your story. For now, I just want you to think more broadly about what obstacles stand in your protagonist's path.

Protagonist Exercise #3

As before, answer the following questions in the third-person voice.

- What actual things or tangible obstacles are getting in the way of what the protagonist wants?
- What emotional obstacles hamper the protagonist? For example, what is the biggest worry, concern, or fear? Explain.

4. What's at Stake?

How intense is the hero's motivation? Ideally, novelists want their protagonists to be motivated by the highest stakes possible, at least within the character's terms. The extremes to which a character is willing to go, and the risks they are willing to take, to overcome obstacles and succeed usually rides on how much the character cares. Are there times in your life when you didn't quit, even though you were totally exhausted, because you wanted something so badly? Conversely, are there times when lack of motivation caused you to give up something you wanted, such as a desire to lose weight?

Usually, our understanding of what we have to lose and what we stand to gain is what inspires us to overcome the obstacles in our path. For example, we may lazily indulge our "sweet tooth," or we may fear facing the hurt feelings that drive emotional eating, and so we never stick to diets. But if our doctor tells us we're obese, and our health is at stake, we may do more, perhaps whatever it takes, to cut those carbs and be healthier.

Inquiring what's at stake helps us clarify what we care about. Another way to ask this question is to consider the consequences if you let the obstacles you identified above keep you from moving forward. Sometimes, we make hard choices and triumph over adversity because our personal integrity is on the line or maybe the welfare of our children. Whatever the reason, clarifying what's at stake can help motivate us to make important changes in our story that we didn't know were possible.

Protagonist Exercise #4

Again, please answer the following questions in the third-person voice.

- What does the protagonist have to lose if he or she fails to act?
- What does he or she have to gain by overcoming obstacles?
- Who and what does the protagonist care most about?
- What would happen if the protagonist let obstacles stand in the way of pursuing what he or she wanted?

Your Protagonist May Surprise You

Congratulations! Now that you have completed all these steps, you should have a deeper understanding of who you are as a multidimensional character.

However, that doesn't mean that you know everything about your protagonist and can predict exactly what he or she will do. Sometimes, authors find that their protagonists take the narrative in unexpected directions as they experience amazing growth and adventures.

The same is true in real life. While creating your character sketch, you may discover surprising new dimensions of your protagonist's personality. That's a good thing — after all, being able to look at the character you play from a novel perspective is a positive first step toward transforming your story. There's more of that to come in the next two chapters, as you explore the roles and scripts that tend to support or undermine your best self.

CHAPTER FOUR

THE ROLES WE PLAY

Some authors start out thinking they know where a story is going to go, only to discover that the main character's natural unfolding takes the plot somewhere else. Suddenly, it's as if the protagonist's drives and need for expression usurps the author, and the writer can't help but move in the direction that the protagonist insists on going. The challenge is, of course, being able to let go.

The same is true in real life. Once you have a sense of where your character arc is headed, you might realize (as Seymour did in the previous chapter) that if you continue following the current trajectory, you won't end up where you want to be. When this happens, you need to be willing to let go of your attachment to who you think you are in order to step into the person — or in this case, the character — you were meant to become.

For example, you may be a marketing professional with an interest in photography. And you may have a sense that your character arc involves developing your creative side by taking a digital photography class. But you might not expect where this will lead: that the photography teacher, seeing "real talent," will invite you on a photography expedition to the Galapagos, and that on this trip, you'll meet your soul mate, who will invite you to live with him in Santa Fe, where you become a wife, a stepmother, and a freelance photographer who occasionally shows in galleries. Of course, this is not what you ever envisioned; it's better.

Naturally, letting go of who you are, and how you expect your narrative to read, is sometimes easier said than done. Once you've built a world around the people, activities, practices, and roles that define you, it can be very difficult to disengage when circumstances change, even for the better. But by closely examining the roles we play, we can determine whether they support or undermine our flourishing.

One of the challenges of being human is giving everything we've got to the characters we're playing, knowing that eventually we may have to let go of the roles we think define us. In fact, once you create your character sketch, you may notice that your protagonist fits, and probably embraces, a number of roles, such as spouse, parent, daughter, and artist. Some roles we eagerly pursue because they provide us with a sense of identity, self-esteem, and perhaps a venerated status, like a doctor or a lawyer. We choose these roles consciously and unconsciously, and for both altruistic and self-serving reasons — to express our unique skills and talents, to improve our financial prospects, to fulfill societal expectations, to win other's admiration, and sometimes to put our values into action. Hence, roles provide a sense of purpose, love, security, status, or a steady paycheck while suggesting certain competencies and intrinsic values — for example, that research scientists are intelligent and mothers are nurturing. Over the course of our story, we are constantly adding roles, which themselves evolve: for example, we all start as children, but we may also become a spouse and a parent, and with each addition the previous roles can shift in nature.

Some roles can feel intrinsic to our identity, and we can have a hard time letting them go or making necessary adjustments when they change. Consider your own story. When has this happened with you? Was it when you realized that you were no longer a child and needed to support yourself financially? Or was it the moment your youngest child left for college? Such transitions can feel daunting.

Yet when we confuse the essence of who we are with the roles we're playing, we run the risk of getting lost when life circumstances change, as they do all the time. In fact, people often seek my counseling services when the roles they identify with are threatened, changing, or taken from them. Sometimes these transitions are welcome, despite some ambivalence, and people simply require time to become acclimated to their new status, such as when parents, after the kids leave home, become empty nesters, or when retirement arrives. More difficult to accept are lost roles due to tragedy or other difficulties — divorce, unemployment, the death of a loved one.

The Self Beyond the Role

When people take charge of their narrative and become protagonists of their own story, I encourage them to regard these role transitions as important parts of every narrative — it's what characters in stories do. Our stories are constantly changing, and our roles along with them. The important thing to remember is that we don't cease to exist simply because the roles we thought defined us are no longer relevant.

This point is illustrated in an interview I read many years ago with Oscar-winning actor Kirk Douglas in a book on Kabbalah, the school of Jewish mysticism. While discussing his approach to acting, Douglas explained that, while he invests enormous amounts of love and energy into the roles he plays, he never completely becomes the characters. The book's author, a rabbi who was also Douglas's Kabbalah instructor, went on to say that we are much more than the roles we assume in life; rather, we are souls playing a part in a larger epic.

It can be hard to see ourselves through such a panoramic lens when we're stuck in a role, especially one that confines us. But when we view our lives from the perch of the third-person narrative, we might just catch a glimpse of ourselves either as actors playing roles or perhaps as souls playing roles that never completely define us. With this in mind, one might even describe the third-person narrative, sometimes referred to as the omniscient narrative, as a spiritual perspective.

After all, the essence of who we are is larger than any single role or roles; as authors of our lives, we are always more than the characters we imagine ourselves to be playing. Additionally, the challenges and opportunities presented by almost every story force us, the protagonist, to evolve in order to meet them. To do so, we sometimes need to enlarge what may be a limited vision of ourselves; that is, we may find that the character we are playing is inadequate, underwritten. Depending on the choices we make, new situations may wake up latent aspects of our character, leading us into territory we never imagined exploring.

Suppose, for example, you leave your career as a successful executive to become a stay-at-home mother. As much as you enjoy your career, you want to be around as much as possible to raise your child, and you can't do both well. So you arrange your finances to accommodate this, and you shelve the competitive, savvy part of your personality for the time being, assuming you'll come back to it. While the transition isn't easy at first, you come to enjoy playing the role of mother and homemaker; you relish developing your nurturing side, and you feel more loving and expansive as you devote yourself to others and a purpose larger than yourself. Eventually, though, it comes time for the child you have raised to leave the nest. Now what do you do? You can't pick up your career where you left off, but do you return to your professional life and resurrect that old role in some form, as you originally intended? Or do you evolve in a new direction, perhaps exploring more seriously a talent and passion for cooking that you discovered, which is now possible in your new role as an "empty nester"?

Framed this way, letting go of old roles is how we free ourselves to explore new ones or reclaim those parts of ourselves we've neglected. The trick is to define ourselves loosely enough to allow for positive change.

Role Exercise

In whatever format you like, in either story or explanatory form, answer all the following questions in the third-person narrative.

1. What are all the roles the protagonist plays in your story? Feel free to make names up if these don't fit traditional roles or labels.

2. Now rank these roles in terms of importance. It's okay if some of them are tied in terms of importance. What do you notice?

3. What is the protagonist's favorite role? What does

the protagonist gain by playing this part? What does this role demand, and what parts of his or her personality does this role express? Explain.

4. What, if any, sacrifices must the protagonist make to play this role? What gifts or parts of his or her personality get temporarily shelved in order to focus on this role?

5. Suppose, for whatever reason, the protagonist could no longer play his or her most favorite part.

    a) How might the protagonist apply the gifts and strengths this role requires in new ways?

    b) What new role would be appealing and help him or her stretch as a person?

    c) Are there old roles the protagonist might revive or gifts he or she might reclaim?

    d) What other aspects might the protagonist develop if given the chance?

CHAPTER FIVE

WHO'S WRITING YOUR SCRIPT?

Sometimes the roles we play, and their societally prescribed scripts, don't really serve us. Yet we keep acting them out simply because we've become accustomed to playing certain characters. Much as we long to flip our scripts, many of us continue to cling to the same, familiar, self-defeating internal monologues that we learned from our parents, peers, teachers, and other characters who were instrumental in shaping our story.

Out of habit, fear, or a lack of imagination, we unknowingly cast ourselves in the same roles — the unrequited lover, the unappreciated spouse, the prodigal son, the exploited employee — because the territory is familiar and our lines are practically memorized: "I'm not good enough." "You don't care about me." "You don't appreciate me." We may also be tempted to adopt a negative storyline that seems to serve us: we justify our situation, and play the victim, by believing "nothing is fair," "I don't have any other options," and "the universe is out to get me." These kinds of stories strain our ability to cope and can take on a life of their own by perpetuating negativity and pessimism.

We first learn certain scripts as young children, when we are most susceptible to messages from parents, siblings, peers, teachers, the media, and other powerful influences in our communities. This continues in adolescence, even though this is a time when children typically question the powers that be. Throughout our lives, we can be influenced by scripts written by others, even when these are incompatible with who we want to be, and sometimes we adopt these scripts without questioning whether they make sense, who's really writing them, and whether or not we're right for the roles.

When we neglect to examine our scripts carefully, we run the risk of living perfunctory or fictitious existences that leave us feeling like strangers to our authentic selves. This can manifest in the following two ways: playing an ill-fitting role and having a poorly written script.

Julia's Story: Playing an Ill-Fitting Role

Sometimes, familial expectations and societal values lead people to choose careers, lifestyles, or partners that are out of sync with their authentic talents and interests. It's like buying a sweater that looks good in a magazine. The sweater complements the model in the pictures, highlighting his or her coloring, lines, and features. But if we become fixated on how happy and desirable the model looks, we might fail to recognize that the same sweater is wrong for us: the color and shape don't flatter our skin tone or our body.

A good example of this is Julia, who was a bright, happily married, thirty-two-year-old attorney and mother of a toddler when I met her. She decided to explore this story writing process because, although she was living the American dream, she struggled with conflicting feelings about her dual role as a working mother and with her frustration that she wasn't "living up to her potential."

While completing the writing exercises, Julia recognized that she was playing the role of "lawyer," but it didn't fit and never had. She'd originally pursued the legal profession because it offered prestige, financial remuneration, and an opportunity to use her highly active mind. Plus, many of her overachieving friends were applying to law school and encouraging her to do the same. However, even just a few months into her legal studies, she had known she had made the wrong choice. She hated it. Still, she had plodded along, passed the bar, gotten married, secured a good job, and given birth to a son.

Now, even with all the outward trappings of success, Julia confessed to being unhappy and unsure what to do. She felt envious of her friends' professional satisfaction and guilty about spending so much time away from her child. Julia was in the coveted position of being able to quit her job because her husband had the means to support the family, yet she chose to work anyway because she saw her friends seamlessly navigating career and motherhood, and she thought she might get bored as a stay-at-home mother. Further, she felt a sense of shame about this last fear because, after all, weren't stay-at-home mothers supposed to be completely content?

On the other hand, Julia recalled how, as a child, she had always been happiest being creative. Her teachers had always praised her musical abilities — she could sing beautifully and play songs on the piano by ear. Yet her working-class parents demonstrated little enthusiasm for Julia's creative talents.

Instead, they encouraged her to get good grades in academic subjects.

Asked to explore the scripts she was following, Julia recognized that most of them weren't written by her:

- The script from her parents told her to value academic and career success over self-expression and personal satisfaction.
- The script from her friends and social milieu "sold me on law school," despite her dislike of practicing law.
- The societal scripts about motherhood sent conflicting, unhelpful messages — that women should effortlessly juggle career and motherhood or else should feel completely satisfied being a stay-at-home mother.

Julia came to see that she wanted to embrace a new script, one that said, "It's okay for me to live life on my own terms." Eventually, she quit her job to devote more time to her son, which included piano lessons for both of them.

Albert's Story: A Poorly Written Script

Sometimes internalized negative messages — "You'll never succeed at anything"; "You must do everything perfectly or not at all" — may prevent us from stepping into and mastering roles that highlight our natural abilities. When they go unchallenged, these messages may unconsciously run our lives, preventing us from enjoying and embracing our blessings. In this case, to continue the sweater analogy, the sweater we bought is actually flattering on us, but we don't see that because we are hyperfocused on our flaws, whether imagined or exaggerated. In other words, the sweater is fine, but the mirror is distorted.

Albert is a good example of this. When he came to see me, Albert was a young aspiring artist who spiraled into self-doubt about his talents whenever teachers at his art school gave him even the mildest of critiques. The same thing also happened whenever fellow students were critical of artists he admired. He worried that if people didn't like the portfolios of clearly talented individuals, no one would ever accept his work. As a result, despite receiving encouragement from his art professors, Albert constantly entertained thoughts of quitting school.

Asked to explore his scripts, Albert traced his doubts back to his father, who had little regard for art that wasn't prominently displayed in a world-class museum. Unconsciously, Albert had internalized the script, "Everyone must think I'm a brilliantly talented artist or I don't belong in this field."

Recognizing that this script was only making him feel discouraged, he decided to embrace a new script that said, "If what I create is an expression of my authentic self and my vision of truth and beauty, whether it is good or bad is irrelevant."

Rewriting Your Script

Many of us can't imagine ditching our negative scripts until we've thoroughly exhausted both our role and our lines. Even then, it takes both insight and dedication to rewrite our story. Where, we might wonder, does one even start?

Initially, we need to clearly identify what negative scripts are running our lives. Next, we need to imagine new, more inspiring scripts. I'll describe this more later, but one simple way to begin is to turn negative language into positive affirmations: take the script "I'll never succeed" and make it "I am good enough"; turn "no one loves me" into "I am lovable"; and transform "what I think doesn't matter" into "I am important."

At first, it might not feel comfortable or authentic to rewrite your script in this way, but give yourself time to grow into it.

Remember, change takes time, determination, and self-awareness. Following negative scripts is why we repeat unhelpful patterns in our lives. Once we understand our "protagonist" better, and identify what he or she really wants, we can write a new script that works better. For now, I want you just to become aware of antiquated scripts and begin considering how you might alter them.

Script Exercise

Please answer the following questions in the third-person narrative. You might imagine how these scripts might read if they appeared in a Hollywood movie about your protagonist's life. What would the protagonist say in the face of adversity? Disappointment? Success? Where were these responses learned, and what positive attitudes or affirmations does your protagonist still need to learn?

1. What scripts did the protagonist learn in childhood?
2. Which one or two of these scripts seem to be getting in the protagonist's way of playing his or her best self? Would you describe them as poorly written, ill-fitting, or neither? Explain.
3. What new scripts might he or she embrace?

CHAPTER SIX

NAMING AND DESCRIBING YOUR CHAPTER

In the 2006 blockbuster movie *The Pursuit of Happyness*, Chris Gardner is a suddenly single father who battles homelessness and ridiculous odds to earn a coveted entry-level position at a major San Francisco brokerage firm. Based on a true rags-to-riches story, the film's narration is divided into chapters with gritty little headings like "Locked Out," "Being Stupid," and "Riding the Bus," which capture the struggles he faces at every turn of his journey. The genius of this film is that twenty-seven of the twenty-eight chapters are about "pursuit," and only the last chapter, as the narrator points out, is entitled "Happiness."

Think about this: If Gardner had gotten stuck in any of those initial twenty-seven chapters, misinterpreting his temporary difficulties as a never-ending story of struggle and victimization, he might have failed to muster the courage and resilience to succeed. Consequently, the film might have been called "Giving Up" and lost one of its central messages — that the seeds of happiness are often sown with toil.

When people become discouraged, it is usually because they mistake one or more difficult chapters in their lives for the totality of their story, the entire plotline. They don't recognize the incremental, purposeful lessons at each passage that can help them move their story forward. That's why, in this chapter, I will guide you in framing your narrative — both in your writing and your mind — as a chapter or episode before delving into the more challenging aspects of your story (which we will do in subsequent chapters).

Sure, life isn't as tidy as novels, which have clearly defined beginnings, middles, and endings. But that doesn't mean that you can't identify smaller plotlines within your larger ongoing story. Doing so helps you examine what each of these narratives has to teach you. Framing your narrative as a chapter means bookending certain events or an era of your life — which can be any period of several months to a year, or maybe even a few years — with a beginning and an end. This encapsulates a particular cause-and-effect sequence of events. Perhaps you just had your first child, and your life has been transformed by a wonderful little person demanding all of your time and attention. Alternatively, maybe your children have fled the nest, or maybe the person you've been living with has just said that he or she only wants to stay together if, eventually, you know you want to have children, and you need to decide what to do.

Thinking of your life episodically has several benefits. First, when life feels overwhelming, knowing that every chapter has an end keeps problems in perspective. Are you going through a rough patch in your marriage? Having a tough time at work? You might tell yourself, "It's just a chapter; this too shall pass." Second, once you've isolated a particular moment in time, with a defined beginning and end, you create a focal point for deeper narrative exploration. When you put this slide of life under the story microscope, you can examine more closely the hidden tensions in your plotline, targeting areas that need care and attention. From there, you can use the third-person voice and your newly acquired understanding of story dynamics to transform old, self-defeating scripts into empowering, redemptive narratives.

Framing your story as a chapter makes story exploration more manageable, and so does naming it. Naming, after all, is both an act of delineation and interpretation. When you name something, you set it apart from other things and define it on its own terms. Naming can be especially helpful during particularly stressful chapters, when circumstances feel confusing and blurry. One of the goals of psychotherapy is to help people name their problems; once something is named, it can be examined, claimed, and situated in a larger context. Indeed, titling each chapter helps name that larger context. For example, recall the story I tell in the preface of my father's passing. While I could accurately title this chapter "Another Heartbreaking Loss" or "Orphaned in Midlife," those titles make me feel sad and sorry for myself. I'd rather use something like "The Prodigal Daughter: A Story of Love, Loss, and Redemption." That has a more positive tone that makes me, ultimately, feel better about the experience. I'm not distorting the truth. I'm simply choosing to interpret my story by emphasizing the redemptive aspects, which gives it meaning in the larger context of my storyline. This chapter isn't only about love, nor only about loss, but about the positive resolution of a difficult passage in my narrative.

The Present as a Starting Point

By this point in your life, you've likely lived through many different chapters. Perhaps you are eager to identify and name them. That's great. I want you to bottle up that enthusiasm and save it for chapter 16, when you will have a chance to review the entirety of your life through this story lens.

For now, I want you to embrace the present — specifically, to focus your attention on the current chapter of your narrative. The present, after all, is a place of power where change becomes possible. It is the precise moment in the story when you, as the protagonist of your story, can take action and grow.

The present is a rich source of information about who you are, where you've been, and where you're heading. By embracing the current moment, you can identify places that often trip you up and take your story in a whole new direction. Right now, is the protagonist tired of being single? If the current chapter is about singlehood, perhaps the protagonist has an opportunity to cultivate self-love by developing talents and healing childhood wounds. Further, perhaps these things *need* to happen before the next chapter arrives, one called "Committed" or "Married."

In his groundbreaking work *The Power of Now*, Eckhart Tolle explains, "Nothing ever happened in the past; it happened in the Now. Nothing will ever happen in the future; it will happen in the now."[15] Everything you've ever done has brought you to the crossroads of this moment. Whatever is puzzling you, or weighing you down, is affecting you in the here and now.

That's not to diminish the value of revisiting the past, whether to reframe a difficult chapter as an important learning experience, to heal old wounds, or to achieve greater self-understanding. There's a time, a place, and a context for such important work. Yet there are pitfalls, too. For instance, we can get bogged down in old storylines — instead of visiting the past, we might pitch camp there or continue to circle the same old beaten tracks. We sometimes focus on the past to the point of distraction, overlooking opportunities in the here and now to transform our story.

This is the beauty of this process: once we name our current chapter, distinguishing it from previous chapters within our larger narrative, we may see how the present moment offers possibilities to embrace a new reality and further develop our character. This new awareness can help us get a fresh perspective on areas where we might feel stuck, reframing life's inevitable trials and tribulations as purposeful experiences that won't last forever.

Plot Summary Exercise

In this exercise, you will write a plot summary of the current chapter of your life. The Plot Summary Exercise is this book's cornerstone exercise. It sets up the remainder of the writing exercises and will become the focal point of your transformational work; I refer back to it often. You will use it to play with your story's mood and tone, identify the antagonist, and explore how narrative tension creates opportunities for character development and attitudinal change.

Because this exercise is so important, I strongly encourage you to keep it close at hand as you complete all subsequent exercises. Of course, the world won't end if you don't. You won't be struck by lightning if you lose your original plot summary, nor will tragedy descend if you revise this summary later, if what seems important today becomes not-so-important tomorrow. However, you'll end up with a much more coherent narrative, and get more juice from the exercises, if you consistently focus all your story exploration around one narrative chapter, namely, the present chapter you are about to describe. If you follow the guidelines, your chapter summary should be far-reaching enough to encompass any shifting tides or bright inspirations in the exercises that follow.

After reviewing the guidelines below, please answer the following two-part question in the third-person narrative:

1. If you were reading the story of your life in a novel, the current chapter would be called, "_____" [insert title], and that chapter would be about _____ [summarize chapter].

Plot Summary Guidelines

Below, I have included two examples of this exercise as a guide. Also keep the following things in mind as you write:

- Your chapter description can be as long as you'd like, but please write at least eight to ten sentences.
- Your description should have a broad-stroke feel that captures the essence of the current era of your life — at least the last few months and up to a year or so. It should read almost like the Cliff Notes version of this chapter.
- Feel free to play with a couple of chapter titles and select the one that feels right. If a better idea comes to you later, you can always change it.
- If it helps you adopt a third-person perspective, consider calling yourself by a nickname or a pseudonym

that has some personal meaning. There is no right or wrong choice.

Example #1: "My Boss, the Queen of Sheba: Surviving a 9-to-5 Dictatorship"

This chapter is about a promising, talented young copywriter in an advertising agency whose ideas are constantly being squashed by a territorial, micromanaging boss. Until now, she has always been fairly lucky...or just gifted. She wasn't entirely sure. Between her portfolio from her college internship and her connections, she secured a foothold in the industry at just the right time. She grew tremendously under the wings of her two previous bosses, who nurtured her creativity and encouraged her to take risks. But this boss, her majesty, is an entirely different species, a character out of the The Devil Wears Prada, *except she sports pants suits from Talbots. "It's just not quite there, Alexandra, it needs a bit more ʒing." Argh! She takes comfort in her amaʒing boyfriend, who puts up with all her kvetching (and occasional panic attacks), treating her to sushi and a foot massage when she's had an especially bad day. What a saint!*

Example #2: "Sally in the Empty Doghouse"

This chapter is about a sixty-four-year-old married woman who is feeling a bit rudderless. She's finished working in her "real" job. Her youngest child just fled the coop (hard to imagine her baby in college!), and her older ones have their own lives. Mornings are especially difficult because each day requires more planning just to stay rooted. Sometimes, she volunteers at a local animal shelter. Other times, she retreats to her ceramics studio in the garage, where she can, in moments, lose herself at the potter's wheel.

But lately, she finds her mind spinning around the same upsetting, fearful thoughts over and over. She feels really isolated, and if she is honest with herself, ashamed at her lack of usefulness. Sometimes she wonders if this four-bedroom house, now empty, should be turned into a commune or perhaps a home for dogs. If only she could convince her husband to get just one dog! Perhaps it's pointless to even ask. She knows she's been wasting a lot of time browsing furniture websites in her quest to redecorate the living room, when what she really needs to do is redecorate her life. It almost feels like she's playing a game, pretending she has important things to do when, in fact, nobody would notice if she stayed home for week to watch every episode of Mad Men. *She has considered returning to teaching high school, but perhaps she should consider a new career. But who would hire her? Is she too old? What does it mean to be in your sixties and out of the workforce? She's scared and discouraged.*

A Time and a Place: Your Setting

Another way of looking at your present chapter is through the lens of setting. Every story is set in a time and place where the events unfold. Both the physical setting, whether it's New York City or a rural African village, and the particular ethos of the times play instrumental roles in shaping the hero's character, in both positive and negative ways.

This is also true in life. For instance, my story includes six major setting changes since my birth, each of which has influenced my character in both subtle and significant ways. My early years in Boston best explain why I occasionally drop the "r" when pronouncing words like "drawer." Growing up in a small New York City neighborhood with a large Sicilian immigrant population fostered my appreciation for family, community, the arts, and good pizza. Studying English at a Vermont party school nourished my critical thinking skills, and it made me realize that I make a terrible sorority girl. Spending my twenties in San Francisco cultivated my independent spirit and appreciation for alternative lifestyles and spiritual perspectives. Living in Baltimore in my thirties nourished my sense of community, roots, and hospitality, as well as my respect for tradition. And every time out-of-town visitors from these different settings ask me to slow down as I'm sprinting up the street, I'm reminded how Manhattan has brought out my latent type-A personality.

These are overgeneralizations, but the point is that no character evolves in a vacuum. We're all affected by our surroundings. Whether or not we are a good fit for those surroundings is another question. The annals of literature — and the offices of psychotherapists, for that matter — are filled with societal misfits who, like Dorothy Gale, long for the other side of the rainbow. Not everyone thrives in the same place. In this regard, people are a lot like plants. Just as a cactus won't survive where a palm tree flourishes, your capacity to prosper is often determined by whether or not your environment provides the proper nourishment and conditions for growth.

In terms of setting, you've already established the time where your story takes place — the present moment. In the next exercise, you'll explore the physical setting of your story, reflecting on whether the environment in which you're currently planted is serving you.

Setting Exercise

Please answer the following questions in the third-person voice.

1. How has setting played a role in the protagonist's story? How has place shaped him or her?
2. What conditions does the protagonist need in order to thrive? For example, does he or she need a small-town vibe, a progressive environment, good public schools, or easy access to nature and outdoor activities?
3. Consider the role of setting, both the times and the physical place, in the current chapter. How does the setting meet the protagonist's needs? How does it fall short?
4. If the setting is falling short, how might the protagonist create a thriving environment without changing his or her setting? How might or could the setting be changed to foster positive growth?

CHAPTER SEVEN

DOOM OR BLOOM: EXPLORING THE POWER OF SPIN

Now that you've summarized the current chapter of your life, it's time to explore your particular storytelling style. How did you spin the story you wrote? Do you tend to see the glass half-full or half-empty?

Generally speaking, society frowns on spin doctors, those shifty hacks and flacks who shape the way politicians, celebrities, and big corporations are presented to the public. We mistrust spin doctors because we know they are trying to manipulate our political and purchasing choices. But the power of spin can also be used for good, especially when we use it to find the positive, redemptive meaning in our narrative by reframing challenges as opportunities to strengthen our emotional, mental, and spiritual muscles so that we can embody our best self. Doing this with the life chapter you summarized in chapter 6 will be the focus of the rest of this book. But first, we will look at the benefits of balancing objective and subjective storytelling and at how the words you choose affect the mood and tone of your narrative.

Triumph or Tragedy: How We Tell Our Stories Matters

Both consciously and subconsciously, we spin our stories all the time. We do this to reflect who we imagine ourselves to be and to influence the impressions others have of us. In fact, how we tell our stories — to our children and to our friends, to strangers and to ourselves — is the determining factor in our worldview and happiness. It influences all our most personal decisions, like who will be our spouse and what will be our career.[16]

Of course, we can leverage the power of spin to work for us or against us. When we spin our stories in counterproductive directions, such as by misreading and misinterpreting the people and events in our lives, we can potentially undermine ourselves. In fact, how we tell our story not only matters; it can mean the difference between whether we view our life as a senseless nightmare or a meaningful experience that leaves us all the wiser.

To illustrate this point, carefully read the following two summaries of *The Wizard of Oz*. When you're done, ask yourself: Which version would you prefer to tell if you were Dorothy? Which version would sustain you through good and bad times? Which one would you prefer as your personal legacy?

The Wizard of Oz: Yellow Brick Nightmare

A young Kansas farm girl who feels ignored and unappreciated by her guardians runs away from home, only to be swept up by a tornado and taken far away.

When she lands, she accidentally kills an evil witch and is then pursued by her homicidal, vengeful sister, an even-more-powerful sorceress. While the girl makes a few friends, they are clueless and don't know their own strengths, and they advise her to place her life in the hands of a fraudulent wizard. The girl does get back home, but only because of some magical slippers she had the whole time. In fact, she could have returned home anytime she wished, and spared herself from this horrific, life-threatening journey, but no one told her until it was over. Even worse, once she finally returns home, none of her relatives believe her, and they think her adventure was just a nightmare. Almost nothing about her circumstances has changed.

The Wizard of Oz: No Place like Home

A young Kansas farm girl who feels ignored and unappreciated by her guardians runs away from home, only to be swept up by a tornado and taken far away. When she lands, she accidentally kills a wicked witch and is then pursued by her homicidal, vengeful sister, an even-more-powerful sorceress. While initially lost, alone, and afraid, the girl receives guidance from a good witch and makes several new friends who dedicate themselves to helping her. Together, they discover they are all stronger then they thought during their hazardous, death-defying journey to visit what turns out to be a fraudulent wizard. At first, she is disillusioned when the wizard cannot help her get home. But eventually the girl realizes she contains within herself all she needs, though she never would have learned this without the devotion of her friends or the challenges that called her to harness the courage, strength, and love she already possessed. Using magic slippers she had the whole time, the girl returns home, where she wakes surrounded by loved ones. Even though they don't believe that the girl ever left Kansas, it doesn't matter. The girl's world has been transformed by her renewed appreciation of her life and family and the awareness of her own personal power.

Fortunately, we can change the way we feel about our story by changing the way we tell it. This is one of the goals in psychotherapy. Often, people become wedded to one version of their story, and they overlook important details that, if included, would improve their perception of their life. One of the underlying principles of narrative psychotherapy is that healing becomes possible when people focus on the parts of their narrative that support their well-being. Toward that end, let's explore the difference between the inner and the outer story.

The Inner and the Outer Story

In my therapy practice, I have a client, Alice, who always wants to give me a play-by-play account of every challenge she experienced over the course of the previous week. She would go on and on, reporting what occurred like the five o'clock news, if I didn't ask her pause to consider those annoying self-reflective questions like, "How do you feel about what happened?" and "What does such-and-such mean to you?" Alice needs someone like me to ask her these questions because, left to her own devices, she'd remain focused only on her outer story. On the one hand, her ability to remain matter-of-fact about the things that happen in her busy life often serves her well as a successful executive and mother of two, but on the other, this means she often tunes out her feelings, which just as often gets her into trouble in her relationships and in her marriage.

Another client, Cathy, has a similar but opposite tendency. She usually focuses too much on her inner story, on her feelings and her subjective interior experience. She does this so excessively that I often have to stop her to ask all those pesky, annoying questions about what actually happened. Once triggered, her emotions are more important to her than the events themselves, and she needs someone like me to help her differentiate facts from feelings and to help her identify emotional embellishment or exaggeration. For example, despite positive job evaluations and steady salary increases, Cathy tends to feel inadequate at work, but the only "objective" evidence of her supposed ineptitude tends to be minor errors or mistakes. Thus, one thing we often discuss is how her tendency to be self-critical (or her inner story) often distorts her perception of her actual performance (or her outer story).

Whereas Alice tends to place too much emphasis on her outer story, Cathy focuses too much on the inner one. The outer story is essentially focused on external circumstances and "facts"; in theory, it's a neutral play-by-play account of what happens, like a CNN report. The first synopsis of *The Wizard of Oz* above is mostly focused on the outer story. It's not false, but the conclusion that nothing changes in Dorothy's circumstances at the end is an incomplete understanding.

The inner story is one's subjective emotional experience; it refers to our interpretation of events. To identify the inner story, we might imagine that we are reading the thoughts of the protagonist as he or she experiences or makes meaning of the action. For example, the second synopsis of *The Wizard of Oz* above emphasizes the inner story of that runaway Kansas farm girl. Seen from the inside, all the troubles she encounters, the unreliable people she meets, and even the return to her original circumstances are essential for her "transformational" discoveries about inner strength, love, friendship, and courage.

Two Equally Valid Perspectives

Both the inner and outer stories are valid and legitimate versions of events that influence each other in profound ways. Yet they are not always aligned or experienced with equivalent satisfaction. As novelist and screenwriter Chuck Wendig suggests in his blog post "25 Things You Should Know about Protagonists": "A character who karate-kicks all the villains to death reaches a positive outcome in his external story, but his internal story may be one of guilt and strife over the violence caused by his karate-wielding death-hands."[17] This is equally true in real life. Focusing on our outer story, our external circumstances, is essential to our survival, but surviving may still be painful if our inner story, our personal experience, suffers. Success in both realms means we have a roof over our heads and can also sleep peacefully at night.

The cut-and-dry objectivity of the outer story has its place. For instance, science is devoted to understanding the world as it is apart from subjective interpretation. Indeed, even in our own lives, distinguishing objective "facts" that we can't change from feelings that we can is essential for wellness. Cognitive behavioral therapy (CBT), in particular, is based on the premise that irrational thoughts emanating from distorted inner stories are at the root of depression and anxiety. As this book shows, old negative scripts can easily creep into and define our inner stories, skewing our interpretation of the bigger picture. "Feelings are not facts" is a basic tenet of this school of psychology.

As such, our inner experience matters, too, sometimes even more than our external circumstances. For starters, we are each subjective individuals, and we can only identify and know "facts" through the lens of our own unique perspective, which includes our intuition and feelings. This kind of knowing defines our inner story, which is essential for making good choices and achieving intimacy. Our feelings of pain and joy guide us as we consider what to do and what changes to make.

Most of all, for our purposes in this book, the outer story isn't concerned with character development, whereas the inner story celebrates it. Often, when it comes to improving our personal lives, positive external changes are preceded by invisible internal ones. For example, the important shifts in outlook and self-esteem we need to grow or succeed are told through the inner story. Does the protagonist learn to believe in him- or herself, handle new responsibilities, and let go of attitudes that hold the person back? Can the protagonist learn to be satisfied with what he or she already has rather than always long for whatever is missing? Such narratives are sorely needed in a society that often places more emphasis on tangible signs of success — a new job, more money, lots of children — than on personal satisfaction and inner peace. Like Dorothy, we must learn both to be steadfast when the world is uncertain or threatening and to find satisfaction and pleasure even within the confines of our humble everyday life. In other words, the inner story traces the growth and development we are still experiencing inside even when our outer story may appear as bleak as winter.

Desperately Seeking Story Balance

What should we do if we suspect our stories are out of alignment? If you tend to be more outer-story focused, consider paying more attention to your thoughts and feelings about what's happening in your life. Ask yourself whether the ways that you are moving through obstacles and meeting challenges is at the expense of pleasure or feeling connected to others. Are workaholic tendencies taxing your body or relationships? If so, think about writing a new chapter in your story in which the protagonist finds a way to successfully balance work and a fulfilling personal life, perhaps by cutting back hours or taking a vacation.

Conversely, if you lean toward overemphasizing your inner story, you can correct the imbalance by identifying areas of unnecessary drama and focus on the facts. Personally speaking, I tend to focus on my inner story, and I've found that making lists and setting deadlines for myself pushes me to accomplish big goals (such as writing this book). Taking such steps helps me feel better about my ability to actualize my ideas, which enhances my inner story.

Inner and Outer Story Exercise

In this exercise, describe the inner and outer story for your chapter summary, which you wrote for the Plot Summary Exercise in chapter 6 (see page 67). As you do this, reflect on whether your protagonist tends to assign more importance to either the inner story or the outer story. What are the advantages and disadvantages of this particular emphasis? What might the protagonist do or think about to better balance these?

Preferably in list format, please answer the following questions in the third-person narrative:

1. Briefly list the elements that comprise the protagonist's outer story or objective circumstances. What events transpired? What facts are named or described? Do not include the protagonist's emotional experience of these events or any sort of interpretation.

2. Briefly list the elements of the protagonist's inner story. The list should reflect the protagonist's emotional experience and interpretation of the outer story.

Example: Sally's Inner and Outer Stories

As an example, here are two possible lists that could be made for Sally, one of the examples I used in chapter 6 ("Example #2: 'Sally in the Empty Doghouse'," page 69).

Sally's outer story list could include the following:

- *She is a sixty-four-year-old married woman.*
- *She is a retired teacher.*
- *She has three grown children; the youngest just left the house.*
- *She volunteers.*
- *She has to plan her day to give her schedule structure.*
- *Her husband doesn't like dogs.*
- *One of her hobbies is pottery.*
- *She isn't working.*

Here is an example of Sally's inner story:

- *She feels rudderless.*
- *Mornings are hard.*

- *She enjoys ceramics and dogs.*
- *She feels isolated.*
- *She's ashamed at her lack of productivity.*
- *She feels old.*
- *She's scared.*

Playing with Mood and Tone

Once you've distinguished the subjective inner story from the objective outer story, I suggest you explore how word choice affects the mood and tone of your narrative.

In life as in literature, the prevailing emotional atmosphere of the tale is called the mood. Does your story make you want to dance or reach for a box of tissues? Mood is often created indirectly; it describes how the style of writing and the presentation make the reader feel. Depending on the writing, the same event could evoke melancholy, cheerfulness, romance, whimsy, gloom, mystery, excitement, humor, and so on. Consider the very different moods conveyed by these two opening lines: "Serene was a word you could put to Brooklyn, New York. Especially in the summer of 1912," and, "It was a dark and stormy night."[18]

The tone, on the other hand, is the protagonist's attitude about the story's events. Is your protagonist optimistic and hopeful or resigned and pessimistic? An optimistic protagonist or narrator expresses the sensibility that, regardless of what is happening, things will turn out okay. Redemption will come in some fashion; if it's not the quintessential happy ending, then it will be a meaningful resolution where lessons are learned and hardships are understood and put in perspective. The heroic soldier will return home from battle to rejoin his family; the middle-aged single woman will overcome her self-defeating relationship patterns and meet her soul mate. Alternately, a pessimistic narrative suggests that, as Dan McAdams writes, "human beings don't get what they desire, and human intentions are repeatedly foiled over time."[19]

One way to influence the mood and tone of your story so that it becomes more positive is to identify any affective statements, emotional language, and subjective interpretations and consider how different words or phrasing would improve the description of your scenario. For example, suppose a protagonist, a mother, were describing the experience of changing a diaper. The woman said it was "yucky, smelly, and disgusting," and she felt "constantly annoyed" that her "precious sleep was always disrupted" to "deal with this disgusting chore." Most of all, she "couldn't get away" from this "horrible relentless mess." Now, consider how the same protagonist might describe the scene if she also focused on her feelings for the baby and not solely on the inconvenience of diaper changing: Woken from her "X-rated dream about Ryan Gosling," her "resentment melted" as she tended to her "helpless little angel," whose "shrieks" gave way to an "adorable smile," and she realized that this "ongoing, stinky labor of love" wouldn't last forever. One day "her child would be grown" and she would "miss it."

Obviously, this is an exaggeration, but perspective and word choice can create a more positive mood and tone while still keeping things honest. As this shows, sometimes what's necessary is to include information that was excluded before or that was overlooked. In the example, diaper changing remains annoying, even unpleasant, but a wider perspective and all the protagonist's emotions are included. According to the precepts of narrative therapy, every time we tell a story we inevitably leave out events, details, and feelings that, if included in the dominant narrative, might change how we remember an experience.

Here's another example. Let's say someone wrote a chapter summary called "Still Searching for Mr. Right" about a single, middle-aged woman who, having gone out with half the eligible bachelors in New York City, is wondering if she should just reconcile herself to a lifetime of loneliness. Written like that, the mood and tone would undoubtedly be pessimistic and somber. But what if the narrative included other details, such as that the woman has tons of beloved friends, a great job, many cultural interests, and a delicious four-year-old niece? What if she acknowledges the great date a month ago with that recently separated man who wasn't quite ready for another commitment? What if she resolves to only date men who are interested in marriage or to unexpectedly embrace singlehood and explore her reluctance to being alone?

When we look closely, there is often more to the story and another way to spin things.

Mood and Tone Exercise

In this exercise, I invite you to review and finesse the mood and tone of your chapter summary, which you wrote for the Plot Summary Exercise in chapter 6 (page 67).

1. In your current chapter summary, circle all the words and phrases connected to your inner story that suggest a negative mood or tone.

2. In a sentence or two, describe the prevailing mood and tone of the chapter.

3. Consider what different word choices might improve the mood. Are there better, more positive ways to describe the same scenario?

4. Using the outer story list you wrote for the Inner and Outer Story Exercise (page 80), consider which details you might emphasize more or deemphasize to change the mood and tone of the story.

5. Consider the protagonist's perspective and whether you can create a lighter, more optimistic narrative tone by approaching the same topics in a different way. How might you rewrite the chapter's events from a different angle?

6. Explore alternate titles. Does a different title change the reader's understanding of or approach to the story?

7. Rewrite the chapter synopsis in all these ways to change a negative mood or tone. When you're done, reflect on whether these changes affected the meaning of your story.

From Doghouse to Potter's Wheel: Sally's Revision

In chapter 6, I provided an example for a woman, Sally, who wrote the chapter synopsis "Sally in the Empty Doghouse" (see page 69). Here, I'll show how she might transform her story. First, Sally underlines the words that convey a negative tone or mood. Notice that most of these words reflect her inner story.

"Sally in the Empty Doghouse"

This chapter is about a sixty-four-year-old married woman who is feeling a bit <u>rudderless</u>. She's finished working in her "real" job. Her youngest child just fled the coop (hard to imagine her baby in college!), and her older ones have *their own lives. Mornings are <u>especially difficult</u> because each day requires more planning just to stay rooted. Sometimes, she volunteers at a local animal shelter. Other times, she retreats to her ceramics studio in the garage, where she can, in moments, lose herself at the potter's wheel.*

But lately, she finds her mind spinning around the same <u>upsetting, fearful thoughts</u> over and over. She feels <u>really isolated, and if she is honest with herself, ashamed at her lack of usefulness</u>. Sometimes she wonders if this four-bedroom house, now empty, should be turned into a commune or perhaps a home for dogs. If only she could convince her husband to get just one dog! Perhaps <u>it's pointless to even ask</u>. She knows she's <u>been wasting a lot of time</u> browsing furniture websites in her quest to redecorate the living room, when what she really needs to do is redecorate her life. It almost feels like she's playing a game, <u>pretending she has important things</u> to do when, in fact, nobody would notice if she stayed home for week to watch every episode of Mad Men. She has considered returning to teaching high school, but perhaps she should consider a new career. But <u>who would hire her? Is she too old</u>? What does it mean to be in your sixties and <u>out of the workforce</u>? She's <u>scared and discouraged</u>.

Next, Sally describes the mood and tone of what she wrote in a few sentences:

The mood of this story is mostly melancholic. There is a sense of hopelessness and despair. The tone is pessimistic and full of doubt and worry.

Then, Sally begins to transform her story. She focuses on details from her outer story list — her husband, her children, her teaching and volunteering, and her pottery — and she considers how she could expand on them, adding details she'd left out before and choosing different words and a more positive narrative approach or tone. Then, she thinks of a new title.

Here is what Sally wrote:

"Sally at the Potter's Wheel"

When the chapter begins, Sally is sitting at the potter's wheel in her garage. It dawns on her that she started this hobby thirty years ago. In that time, she's had a successful professional career culminating in writing a two-year college program with national accreditation. She's had the pleasure of being a full-time program director at two colleges, and many of her students have gone on to very good careers. She's even been with the same man for thirty-eight years! Her daughters light up her life with their beauty, intelligence, and strength. She's so proud of raising these young women. She's been volunteering in her community for more than twelve years, helping whenever she can and not shrinking from any hurdles she meets along the way.

As she stares at the doughy mass on the wheel, she identifies with the clay — amorphous yet supple, bound to the earth with all its laws of time and gravity. Funny how, when she sits down at the wheel, she is never quite sure what she is going the make. Only after she has begun massaging the doughy mass does the clay reveal whether it wants to be a cup, a vase, or a bowl. She smiles at her epiphany, that she is both the potter and the clay. Not sure

where her life is headed, she pushes down on the wheel's
pedals, feeling the earth spinning beneath her fingers.

Notice how Sally is able to shift both the mood and tone simply by focusing on different aspects of her story. She doesn't need a career counselor, or more furniture, or a husband who likes dogs — nor does she resolve her concerns about her future. Instead, by being more mindful of the content of her story and her word choices, she creates a sentimental, contemplative mood and a more hopeful tone that includes some important insights.

It's worth noting that, in revising her narrative, Sally became more creative with the writing itself; she shifted her perspective to capture a moment of reflection during an activity she enjoyed. Similarly, consider taking an unusual path or another imaginative approach to recasting your narrative; the possibilities are endless. Of course, you don't need to; you can simply revise your plot summary so that it reads like a lighter, more optimistic version of the same narrative. Most of all, write your story in a way that appeals to you. While observing my writing guidelines will keep you from digressing into old, unproductive stories, don't be afraid to step out of your comfort zone and add your own creative touch.

CHAPTER EIGHT

CONFLICT:
THE ULTIMATE CHARACTER WORKOUT

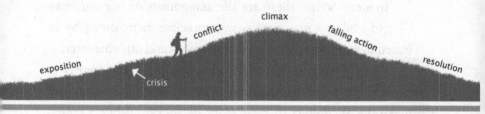

Character cannot be developed in ease and quiet. Only through experience of trial and suffering can the soul be strengthened, ambition inspired, and success achieved.

— Helen Keller, *Helen Keller's Journal*

Conflict: The struggle between two opposing forces — the protagonist and the antagonist — that fuels the engine of a story. This includes the action of the story that gradually builds to a climax.

Have you ever noticed that the same type of character keeps showing up in your life and pushing all of your buttons? These people may look nothing alike or even share the same gender, but they keep presenting you with more or less the same frustrations and issues. Or perhaps it's not a certain person but a certain negative situation that you always find yourself struggling with. Perhaps you're always picking up the slack and yet your contributions are never appreciated. Maybe you keep dating high-maintenance women or neglectful men. Why do these characters and situations keep appearing in your storyline?

In story terms, these are the antagonists of our narrative — and while we may not like or appreciate them, they play an instrumental role in shaping our plotlines and our character.

Usually, when I introduce the concept of antagonists in my writing workshops, people want to know how they can make the antagonist of their story disappear. While I empathize with the sentiment, having entertained similar thoughts myself, I encourage my writers to take a wider view. Instead, I propose a potentially more productive, if not more satisfying, question: "Why has this antagonist or antagonistic situation appeared in my story, and what does he, she, or it have to teach me?" Framed this way, an antagonist presents us with an invitation: When our antagonist shows up, do we run away, turn our heads, or surrender to the way things are while hoping for the best? Or do we rise to meet the challenges, embracing our antagonist as if he, she, or it were a full-body toning instrument designed to open our heart muscles and build up our resistance to the gravity of life? What opportunities for personal growth would we miss if our obstacles simply disappeared?

To answer this question, we need to understand more about the nature of conflicts in stories and the role the antagonist plays in helping the hero of the story stretch beyond his or her perceived limitations.

Character Workouts: Necessary Friction

Because this kind of inner and outer work often requires deep internal stretching and strengthening, I like to consider conflict as the ultimate character development workout.

Many of us don't think twice about pushing ourselves to the point of pain and exhaustion at the gym. Yet when life pushes us to exercise our emotional, spiritual, and mental muscles, we often would prefer lighter, gentler, no-impact routines. Until we are willing to build these character development muscles, we will remain somewhat stunted in our growth, unable to actualize the full strength of what we are capable of, whether in our career, relationships, or communities.

Conversely, the more toned and refined we grow, the easier it becomes to do the emotional heavy lifting and the freer we are from our internal strife. And the freer we are from internal strife, the more energy we have to share our gifts with others.

Unfortunately, character doesn't develop in a vacuum. Life typically presents us with circumstances that test our weaknesses and bump our rough edges. These circumstances, which we call "conflicts" in the world of stories, present us with opportunities to refine these edges or run the risk of becoming...well, even edgier. In the world of fiction, not only do we expect conflicts but also we recognize, consciously or not, that they are an important part of the narrative. When reading a book or watching a film, many of us don't question that hard chapters often leave the sufferer wiser and stronger.

In life, though, the word "conflict" typically has a pretty bad rap. Few people consciously seek conflict, and many people, myself included, will go out of their way and spend a great deal of effort to avoid it. When it comes to our own stories,

when things don't go our way, we tend to question the benevo-
lence of the universe — or, as a friend of mine likes to say, "Oh
great, another *#%! growing experience!"

In life as in literature, conflict is defined by the tension
between the protagonist and an antagonist — which can be a
person, a situation, a force of nature, or even the protagonist
working against him- or herself. Like the process of friction,
the force of resistance between the protagonist and the antagonist creates the kinetic energy that heats up the story, propelling
the characters toward an ultimate confrontation (or climax)
that, more often than not, is resolved with a significant change
in the protagonist's circumstances and/or in the protagonist's
understanding of self and world.

In the classic story structure, this conflict is triggered by a
crisis that upsets the status quo, setting off a chain reaction of
events in the outer story. In *The Wizard of Oz*, for instance, the
crisis begins when the primary antagonist, Miss Gulch (who
later morphs into the Wicked Witch) arrives at Dorothy's
doorstep and takes Toto to be destroyed. These events agitate
the protagonist's inner story, forcing the character to make difficult personal choices. In this case, Dorothy must decide: Does
she stand up to Miss Gulch and Auntie Em to protect her dog,
or does she take Toto and run away from home?

Note, however, that the "crisis" can be either a positive or
negative event that can vary in its degree of apparent serious-
ness. For example, a character may regard getting engaged or
married as a genuinely happy event and still experience a wide
range of challenging crises: a boss who assigns a huge project
during wedding plans, or a controlling mother who wants to
set the guest list and create a huge affair when the protagonist wants a small and intimate ceremony. Can the character

balance work and personal life? Can the character finally say no to Mom? Perhaps the bakery delivers the wrong cake. Can the character learn to let go of the small disappointments that always seem to undermine his or her joy?

Whatever the circumstances, antagonists keep stories from stagnating. They force protagonists to change in necessary ways — to step outside their comfort zones, take a closer look at their emotional reactions, do things differently, and/or make important decisions that will determine how much they grow. In real life, such character development workouts can help us stretch beyond our perceived limitations to discover the true depth of our own capacity to love, succeed, and overcome obstacles. That's not to say that we should seek out conflict for personal growth's sake or use character development as an excuse to endure chronically painful or unpleasant circumstances. Constant pain is a sign that something is amiss. Yet any workout should include a little discomfort so we increase our flexibility to handle more intense situations with greater degrees of ease. It reminds me of something a dance teacher once told me: "Sometimes, when you begin to stretch, your muscles scream 'no, no, no' — they don't think they can handle the tension because it's never been asked of them before. But as you gradually ease into the pose, they relax and discover an untapped capacity for elasticity."

The Four Types of Conflict

In literature, conflict is often divided into four categories or types: self versus other, self versus society, self versus nature, and self versus self. Each conflict is defined by its own particular type of antagonist and crisis. However, as you read these descriptions, if the terms "conflict," "crisis," and "antagonist" feel uncomfortable to you (or don't seem to fit your story), don't get hung up on semantics. Replace these terms with "tension," "challenge," or whatever word you wish. The principles remain the same, and I mean these words loosely to draw parallels with literature. That said, here are the four types of conflict.

1. Self vs. Other

Antagonist: Another person, whether a spouse, boss, colleague, relative, friend, or stranger

Crisis: Something the antagonist does or says that upsets the status quo

Everybody knows this type of conflict. After all, human beings are relational creatures — we live in families and communities and seek out social interactions to expand our awareness about our environments and ourselves. We need others. Yet because we don't all share the same goals, circumstances, or worldviews, we are bound, eventually, to come across someone who pisses us off or challenges our point of view.

Some antagonists in our lives are almost like quintessential "villains" — such as the ex-husband who won't pay child support or the inconsiderate neighbor who throws loud, raucous parties. Yet, more often than not, antagonists are people we know quite well and even love — say a spouse, a sibling, or a parent — who pushes our buttons, triggers our complexes, and inspires us to take ten deep breaths and run around the neighborhood to avoid saying something awful we'll regret later.

We can have mixed feelings when the "antagonist" in our story is someone we care about and want to be with. One woman I worked with identified the antagonist of her story as her artist fiancé. As much as she could scarcely bear being apart from him, she had concerns about his ability to make a comfortable living if she chose to be a stay-at-home mother. In this case, the woman's conflict wasn't so much with her story's antagonist as with her own expectations, and her challenge was to clearly express her needs and desires, clarify her values, choose love over fear, and explore the source of her scarcity issues around money.

Another woman identified her antagonist as her intelligent yet idle twenty-one-year-old son, who lived at home and chose to play video games instead of looking for a job. The woman loved and believed in her son, and she didn't want to kick him out. Rather, she needed to address her inner story, her own expectations and beliefs about parenting, and she had to let go of her ever-present desire to manage her son's life. She needed to learn to set better limits for herself and also to allow her son to fail if necessary, even though that reality was unlikely.

The same principle holds true even if you think your antagonist is just a rotten human being. After all, "rotten human beings" are people, too, and they aren't always rotten. Often, we may be tempted to demonize antagonists, casting them in the role of the villain. This makes it easier for us to justify our victimhood, instead of taking a long, hard, honest look at how our own prejudices, assumptions, expectations, and vulnerabilities may be contributing to the conflict. Typically, we don't like recognizing negative qualities in those we love or positive qualities in those we don't, but the antagonists in our stories frequently cause discomfort precisely because of the moral ambiguity they represent.

One woman identified her antagonist as a verbally explosive boss, and she put it this way: "Knowing there is a kernel of good in him makes my decision of whether or not to quit much more difficult. If he was always a horrible person, I would have an easier time knowing what to do. I just wish he were more like a Disney villain: 100 percent evil. Disney heroes never question the right thing to do. They're faced with something so bad that the right answer becomes obvious."

When we demonize our antagonists, we run the risk of turning our antagonists into one-dimensional characters, forgetting that they too are the star of their own stories, with their own antagonists — one of whom may be us! As the protagonists of their own stories, they have positive motivations, obstacles, and things at stake. As a wise friend of mine once noted, the dragon doesn't know he's the bad guy. He's just trying to protect his little dragon babies and giant pot of gold.

Thus, unlike in fiction, where killing the villain may be all that's needed to metaphorically resolve the conflict, in the stories we write about our life, conflict with people is usually resolved only after we make changes within ourselves. That doesn't excuse someone else's behavior, and occasionally we need to remove people from our lives who treat us badly. But first, almost invariably, we must change our inner story before we can change our outer story.

2. Self vs. Society

Antagonist: A social culture, bureaucracy, corporation, government, or religion

Crisis: A layoff, cultural attitudes, laws or rules, political decisions

Examples of this type of conflict range from struggles for civil, women's, and gay rights to trying to get the cable company to restore our Internet service in a timely manner. In this scenario, the protagonist is one small voice in a million, a cog in the machine, a David taking on Goliath.

Conflict with society often involves a struggle to be our authentic self: the prevailing culture may condemn our values or something intrinsic to our identity, like our sexuality, our skin color, or our religious beliefs. It also often can involve a struggle against negative or oppressive social conditions, like unemployment, poverty, racism, or social convention.

Typically, the antagonist is a group or a way of thinking that pushes the protagonist to make strong moral choices or assert his or her true identity, whether that's acceptable to others or not. Often, the protagonist feels or is alone; he or she may lack the support of friends, family, and community. Consequently, resolving this conflict can take a high degree of inner strength, self-trust, and resolution. Overcoming doubts is essential, as the protagonist must be certain his or her position is worth defending against common opinion. The strength and endurance required for this type of character workout can be intense, since you may feel isolated or face a powerful system capable of harming you. The stakes can be high.

Not every self-versus-society conflict involves dystopian governments or nefarious corporations, however. Your protagonist might be, for example, a sixty-year-old professional who is battling ageism in a highly competitive job market, or perhaps an economic recession has stalled hiring and stagnated wages in his or her profession.

Finally, just as a benevolent individual can play the antagonist in your story, so can benevolent social expectations. Has your protagonist just graduated from college? Congratulations! Now he or she needs a job, an apartment, a car, a life.

This kind of personal growth workout exercises your self-sufficiency muscle, your perseverance, as well as your faith that you will eventually find work in your chosen career, even if, in a highly competitive job market, your profession is outsourcing most of its entry level work to India.

3. Self vs. Nature

Antagonist: A storm, earthquake, wilderness, weather, or the environment

Crisis: A natural event like a hurricane or avalanche, or a disaster like a fire or a shipwreck

Fictional stories often feature self-versus-nature conflicts, which are ripe with drama, but these are less-common scenarios in the work I do. Nevertheless, environmental catastrophes like hurricanes, earthquakes, and storms do happen, and they typically raise issues of powerlessness, humility, and a sense of our insignificance in the grand scheme of things. In the face of this type of antagonist, we often must hone our faith, endurance, intelligence, and ability to marshal all our resources.

Usually, though, even when people have been displaced by major hurricanes and tornadoes, the primary antagonist in their stories isn't the natural disaster itself. In the aftermath, the challenge becomes one of self versus society, as large swaths of the population struggle to rebuild and must sometimes compete for limited relief services and deal with ineffectual or ill-prepared governments. One need only think back to the havoc and devastation wrought by Hurricane Katrina, which exposed government corruption, racism, and classism to see how these two types of antagonists are often inextricably linked.

4. Self vs. Self

Antagonist: The self

Crisis: A physical or mental illness or negative behavior pattern

We all know what it means to struggle with oneself. If you've ever, as they say in twelve-step meetings, made the same mistake over and over and expected different results, then, congratulations, you're a human being. More difficult, though, is when we must cope with a serious mental or physical illness. Because our very bodies and minds betray us, this conflict represents one of the most rugged character workouts there is. Understandably, we typically resent this particular personal trainer. However, this type of workout often strengthens and expands the love and courage muscles, both of which are connected to the heart. Additionally, it tends to work out the clarity muscle, revealing what's important and what's not.

In literature, this category of antagonist is usually referred to as "human versus self." I prefer "self versus self" to emphasize that every conflict is, to some degree, an internal one. After all, your encounters with challenging humans and situations are filtered through your own thoughts and feelings. Whether the protagonist of your story is getting divorced, battling the elements on Mount Everest, fighting for democracy in Egypt, or coming out of the closet, every conflict is ultimately processed in the trenches of one's heart, mind, and spirit. A woman may identify her narcissistic husband as the antagonist, his affair as the crisis, and divorce as the resolution, but she will inevitably face many difficult personal choices. A man battling a tyrannical regime may identify the government as his antagonist, but he will face many moral decisions about what to do, such as whether to risk putting his family in danger or to break laws and risk imprisonment.

In this respect, the self is both the protagonist and antagonist of every story. No one can avoid this conflict, and it is frequently the most important one to resolve.

Identifying the Primary Antagonist

Now it's time to identify the primary antagonist of the current chapter of your story. This writing exercise will serve as the foundation for the next few chapters, where you will identify the emotional muscles being targeted and strengthened through the character workout or conflict of your narrative.

As you were reading about different kinds of conflicts, you may have found yourself identifying more than one antagonist. That's normal. Within any given story, there may be several conflicts and more than one antagonist, and that's not including the self, which can often be considered an additional antagonist in any conflict. For example, consider the woman getting divorced. Her husband is certainly an antagonist, but she may also be struggling with unemployment, her health care coverage, and an exasperating legal system. She might have a financial crisis, conflicts with her kids, and a lost pet. As life would have it, the more antagonists we have in our story, the more stressed we feel.

While in real life it is often necessary to fight fires on many fronts, you will get more out of this story work if you choose one primary antagonist for all of the conflict-related exercises. This should be whoever or whatever is monopolizing your attention right now. In fact, you may have already identified this particular person, thing, or situation, but whether you have or not, do the Primary Antagonist Exercise below to clarify all the antagonists in your story. Remember, you can always do this process again, writing about a different life chapter involving a different antagonist.

In addition, I strongly suggest that you consider all the other possible antagonists — person, society, or environment — before selecting yourself as the primary antagonist. Even if you feel you are your own worst enemy, you will get a richer experience from the writing exercises in the next few chapters if the primary antagonist is someone or something else. For instance, if you feel emotionally or morally conflicted, identify what triggered that internal conflict. If you feel plagued by negative, self-defeating scripts (which you may have identified in chapter 5), consider who or what is behind those scripts. Does someone in your story fit that same character type? Or, if you are suffering from anxiety in anticipation of retiring, then choose retirement, not anxiety, as your antagonist. However, if you examine your story in all these ways and still feel that you are the primary antagonist, then proceed using the central conflict of self versus self.

Primary Antagonist Exercise

Using the revised chapter synopsis you wrote for the chapter 7 Mood and Tone Exercise (see page 84) — along with the inner/ outer story lists (see page 80) — create the chart below and answer the following questions in the third-person narrative. If there isn't a clearly defined conflict in your chapter 7 synopsis, try using the summary you wrote in chapter 6. Remember, you're looking for a point of narrative tension or catalyzing situation that is pushing the hero to stretch beyond his or her current comfort zone. This may or may not be an adversarial situation as classically defined.

First, to identify the primary antagonist, begin by creating a table with three columns: the first labeled "Conflict(s)"; the second, "Explanation"; and the third, "Antagonist(s)." Across each row, describe a different conflict the protagonist faces in the current chapter.

- In the left column, summarize each conflict — for example, "Being unemployed for six months" or "Planning a wedding." Name at least one and no more than five.
- In the middle column, under "Explanation," briefly summarize (in the third-person narrative) the reason for selecting each conflict. If you feel you need more space to write, feel free to do so on a separate piece of paper. However, in my experience, summarizing helps people home in on the issue that's bothering them.
- In the third column, list all the corresponding antagonists associated with each conflict (each conflict or crisis may involve more than one antagonist).

On the next page you'll find an example of what this table might look like. For illustration purposes, I've described four different types of conflicts for four different theoretical protagonists. After all, it's unlikely (but not impossible) that someone would be planning a wedding, getting divorced, looking for work, and facing an empty nest at the same time. However, if you've identified more than one conflict, your chart may look similar to this.

Conflict(s)	Explanation	Antagonist(s)
Planning a wedding	She feels like she has to make a choice between the wedding she and her fiancé want and making everyone else happy. There are also lots of difficult personalities and delicate family dynamics.	1. Mom, who wants a bigger affair than she and her fiancé 2. Estranged sister-in-law (should she be in the wedding party?) 3. Crazy Aunt Betty, who always gets drunk and makes a scene
Unemployment	He hasn't worked in six months and needs to keep up with the mortgage	1. Wife, who is pressuring him to do more 2. Dead father, who never believed in him 3. Bad economy/competitive job market 4. God, who isn't answering his prayers 5. The protagonist himself, who is losing motivation
Empty nest	Figuring out what to do now that her youngest daughter has gone off to college	1. Career 2. Ageism 3. The protagonist, who has lost her sense of purpose and identity 4. Husband, who doesn't want to get a dog
Divorce	Dealing with a difficult spouse; mourning the end of a twenty-year relationship	Soon-to-be ex-spouse

Now it's time to home in on the primary antagonist. If you listed more than one conflict, choose the conflict that is causing the most headaches, heartaches, anxiety, and confusion. (Don't concern yourself with trying to resolve the conflict quite yet — that will be the task of the next few chapters. For now, the purpose is to zero in on an antagonist for further exploration.) With this in mind, answer the following questions in the third-person narrative, preferably in a way that reads like a story:

1. Who is the primary antagonist? What makes the antagonist so challenging for the protagonist?
2. What are the antagonist's redeeming qualities? How do these qualities affect or complicate the protagonist's thoughts and feelings about the situation, if at all? Explain.
3. What is the antagonist's point of view? If so inspired, write the chapter synopsis from the perspective of the antagonist.

Example: Primary Conflict: Planning a Wedding

The primary antagonist is her mother. She feels guilty admitting this because she loves her mother and knows she is lucky to have such a caring one. The problem is, of course, that her mother cares way too much...about everything — the dresses, the guests, the venue, the cake, the caterer, and even more problematic, who's in the wedding party. This last piece is particularly problematic because the protagonist's fiancé doesn't want his estranged sister in their bridal party. The protagonist understands and respects her fiancé's position — as he and his sister have been on chilly terms since she stole some family heirlooms after their father died.

Yet her mother, who was spared these details at her fiancé's request, subscribes rather zealously to the belief that "blood is thicker than water." The protagonist also suspects that her mother is concerned about the family image.

In any event, the protagonist has always been attuned to her mother's moods and needs, and she very much wants her approval. Her mother, after all, is a very admirable person — she not only raised two children and maintained a happy thirty-three-year-marriage, but she also worked as a lawyer. She is used to getting her way and always thinks she is right. The protagonist also recognizes that obsessing over wedding details is her mother's way of expressing love because she wants the best for her daughter.

Still, growing up in the shadow of such a mother, the protagonist had trouble finding her own voice. Today, her mother has trouble seeing her daughter as an adult, even though the protagonist just turned thirty-one! If she's really honest with herself, the protagonist also has trouble accepting her adult status, which is probably why her mother triggers her so much. She and her fiancé very much want their wedding to be an expression of their love and who they are as a couple. They want a small, but tasteful, low-key wedding, while her mother wants a fancy affair that represents the entire family.

Can she stand up to her mother and insist on doing her wedding her own way? And what does she owe her mother as daughter? Can she handle her mother's disappointment or disapproval? This is the essence of her conflict.

CHAPTER NINE

READING BETWEEN THE LINES: EXPLORING CHARACTER STRENGTHS AND VULNERABILITIES

All authors strive to create perfect foils for their protagonists — antagonists that will compel their heroes to marshal their strengths and overcome vulnerabilities in the face of adversity. What if that same dynamic applied to your life's story? What if you have been given — or perhaps have unconsciously created through the choices you've made — the perfect antagonist to push you to become a better, stronger, deeper version of yourself? If conflict is the ultimate character development workout, then our antagonists are the personal trainers who push us beyond our perceived limitations to develop our flabby, underutilized emotional muscles. As with a personal trainer, we might openly swear or grin through gritted teeth. We might assign the person sadistic aspirations, thinking the trainer *wants* to harm or destroy us. But if we read between the lines, the antagonist is just helping us build our strengths while further honing the underdeveloped areas within ourselves. This chapter will help you examine these areas of strength and vulnerabilities more closely.

As anyone who exercises knows, the muscles you use most often are always the strongest. When engaging in physical activity, you may notice how you tend to lean on those stronger muscles to power through challenging exercises. The same is true of our character muscles. When you feel like the circumstances in your life are pushing you to stretch outside your comfort zone, marshaling your strengths — whether they be intelligence, creativity, or a good sense of organization — can help you muster the energy you need to overcome obstacles.

Whether you're aware of it or not, you rely on certain character strengths to perform well in life. Your strengths consist of both talents and skills. Talents are the strengths that come naturally, and we often don't think much about them. Most of the time, we even take them for granted. For example, you might underplay the degree of resilience and resourcefulness it took to survive growing up in a dysfunctional family or, perhaps, the degree of creativity it took to design a beautiful home. Skills are the strengths we develop through practice, repetition, and attention. For example, you may have a talent for music, but as the old saying goes, you won't get to Carnegie Hall as a professional musician if you don't practice, practice, practice.

Acknowledging Strengths

Taking stock of your cumulative strengths can be especially helpful when navigating the central conflict in your story. For instance, a single, middle-aged woman moving to a new city to start her dream job might want to remind herself that she's intelligent, social, creative, and resourceful. This can help her get through those anxiety-ridden nights when she wonders what the heck she was thinking starting over at forty-two.

In this chapter's first exercise, take a moment to reflect on the character strengths you associate with your story's protagonist. If you are having difficulty identifying a particular strength, think back to the last time you did something you were proud of. What strengths did you use to achieve this victory? Also think about what other people notice about you. You might regard your strengths as superpowers, the things you know you can count on to excel in most situations.

Since I sometimes find that people have trouble coming up with strengths, here are some to consider. Obviously, this is not a complete list.

CHARACTER STRENGTHS

Ability to forgive	Insightfulness
Ability to love and be loved	Intelligence
Appreciation of beauty and excellence	Judgment
	Kindness
Authenticity	Leadership
Cooperation	Prudence
Courage	Resilience
Creativity	Scholarship
Curiosity	Self-control
Decisiveness	Sense of gratitude
Empathy	Sense of justice
Enthusiasm	Sense of organization
Equanimity	Sensitivity
Flexibility	Social intelligence
Hope	Spirituality (faith, purpose)
Humility	Tolerance
Humor	Wisdom

Character Strength Exercise

Answer the following questions in the third-person narrative.

1. What are your protagonist's greatest strengths? Explain.
2. Imagine that your protagonist is a superhero. Describe his or her primary superpowers.
3. How might the protagonist marshal his or her strengths (or superpowers) to navigate the primary antagonist in the current chapter of his or her story?
4. In what ways has the protagonist used these strengths to navigate similar challenges in the past? What were the lessons learned? How might they help now?

Embracing Vulnerabilities

It feels good to be strong. Almost by definition, we lean on and use our strengths to succeed in life and overcome obstacles. Figuratively speaking, our strongest muscles hold us up and support our day-to-day functioning. Yet, as any personal trainer will vouch, the areas where we are weakest are the ones that often need the most attention, to improve our overall fitness and reach our full potential. While most of us can probably identify the weaker areas on our physical bodies — be they our abs, biceps, or buttocks — we may be hard-pressed to identify the emotional and mental muscles that could use some strengthening, nor do we devote ourselves to exercising them with the same focus and intensity that we reserve for flabby arms at the gym.

Still, these emotional muscles are essential for optimal human flourishing and an important component of our character development workout. Just as we might begin a regimen of personal training by targeting certain muscle groups, the goal of our next writing exercise is to acknowledge our character vulnerabilities and begin to understand them better. This way, we can focus on and isolate those aspects of ourselves we need to further hone and develop, so we can transform them into assets.

As personal trainers, our antagonists are adept at pointing out to us these less-developed muscles. Antagonists do this both directly and indirectly — sometimes by sharing their opinions or judgments, and sometimes by holding up a mirror that reveals our more vulnerable parts. Usually, vulnerabilities lurk within our inner stories; they reflect our emotional constitution. Remember Milo's story in chapter 1 (see page 15)? A politician's criticism left him feeling doubtful about his abilities. Like Milo, we all have tender areas within our psyche that are especially sensitive to criticism, rejection, or fear of failure. We all have triggers that can plunge us into old scripts about how we're defective in some way (for more, see chapter 5).

That's why, when your primary antagonist points these things out to you, your initial response may be to stick your fingers in your ears or close your eyes. No one wants to face criticism, and we can resent those who force us to acknowledge our vulnerabilities. Sometimes we fear that, if we do so, it means that we will open ourselves up to being perceived as inferior or being taken advantage of. We might also misinterpret what these vulnerabilities mean and draw false conclusions. For example, we might equate doubting our own abilities with proof that we are incompetent. We may even make up stories about what incompetency means — for example, "If I'm incompetent, then I will never succeed in my career...or be loved, appreciated, and admired for my unique contribution to society."

Yet recent studies suggest that society has gotten the story about vulnerability all wrong. In fact, the latest psychological research, popularized by TED Talk phenomenon Dr. Brené Brown, suggests that vulnerability is the key to successful intimate relationships and the secret behind inspired leadership.[20] Acknowledging that we have been hurt or have erred not only helps people trust and feel more connected to us, but also it invites others to open up about themselves. Sharing our vulnerabilities also sends a message to others that it's permissible to make and learn from our mistakes, creating a climate of openness in our professional, social, and family circles.

When considering the relationship between the primary antagonist and vulnerabilities, however, it's important to note that we shouldn't assume that everything an antagonist says or shows us is necessarily accurate or even true. Sometimes, the vulnerabilities our antagonist points out may, in fact, be projections of the antagonist's own vulnerabilities, which the person refuses to acknowledge. But chances are, if you're having some kind of reaction, it is a sign that you have internal work to do. Otherwise, the antagonist of your narrative wouldn't present much of a conflict at all — you'd simply shake the situation off and move on with your day. After all, you know more than anyone else when something strikes a nerve or bumps up against an old unhealed wound.

In fact, the primary antagonist in the current chapter of your story may remind you, either consciously or unconsciously, of other antagonists in your past who helped create or significantly contributed to those wounds. For instance, a man whose current antagonist is just the latest in a string of difficult bosses may have authority issues that trace back to his father. A woman whose recurring antagonists are untrustworthy female friends may have trust issues with her mother.

When this occurs, I encourage you to recognize, or try to identify, any underdeveloped muscles this pattern indicates. The more you pay attention to these areas of vulnerability, the greater opportunity you have to strengthen them, so that you can use them to change your narrative. Acknowledging our vulnerabilities can help us identify what muscles need strengthening. With awareness and practice, we can make new choices in response to the obstacles we face.

Character Vulnerabilities Exercise

Using the chart you created for the Primary Antagonist Exercise in chapter 8 (page 101), create a new chart that lists only the primary conflict and the primary antagonist you identified. In this chart, you do not need the "Explanation" column. However, you can also simply revise the chapter 8 chart and add to it as instructed, if you wish.

Then, add a third column, entitled "Vulnerabilities," and list the vulnerabilities that are being revealed by the protagonist's conflict with the antagonist. You can describe each vulnerability with a single word or a short phrase, and these can be anything; there is no right or wrong type of vulnerability. You can also list as many vulnerabilities as you like; a divorce, for example, could trigger several. However, you only need to list one, and if you get stuck, ask what type of feelings are being exposed or brought to the surface by the crisis. In the example below, I've listed possibilities for each of the four original conflicts.

Conflict	Primary Antagonist	Vulnerabilities
Planning a wedding	Mom	Desire for approval Lack of self-trust Fear of independence Conflicting loyalties
Unemployment	Bad economy / competitive job market	Impatience Easily discouraged Exhaustion Fear of failure Self-doubt
Empty nest	The protagonist	Loneliness Fear of growing old Self-doubt Lack of direction Shame
Divorce	Soon-to-be ex-spouse	Anger Resentment Fear of being alone Guilt Embarrassment

After identifying the vulnerabilities the primary antagonist has targeted for your character workout, answer the questions below in the third-person narrative. Feel free to respond to each question individually or, if you're feeling more adventurous, write a narrative about the history of your vulnerability using the questions as guidelines.

1. What is the history of this vulnerability? How has it shown up in the protagonist's past? How has it gotten in the way of the protagonist's best self?

2. What might be the source of the protagonist's vulnerability — for example, an overbearing or critical parent or perhaps a childhood illness that prevented him or her from engaging in the same activities as other children?

3. What meaning does the protagonist make of the story? For example, does the protagonist assume that self-doubt makes the person unlovable or that being ashamed of getting divorced means that divorce is, in itself, shameful? What might be an alternate, positive interpretation?

4. Has this type of antagonist appeared in your story before? If so, how might you summarize him/her/it in a nutshell? (Example: The benevolent authority figure who often offers unsolicited advice "for your own good.") How does this make the protagonist feel (such as, angry, disrespected, insecure, or infantilized)?

5. If the antagonist is a recurring character type, how has the protagonist historically responded to the challenges he/she/it presents? In what ways has this response been effective (using strengths) and in which ways has it been ineffective (revealing vulnerabilities)?

6. How might the protagonist respond differently in the current situation?

7. Suppose you were asked to create the perfect antagonist to help the protagonist address and overcome vulnerabilities. What would he or she be like and what obstacles or challenges might the antagonist present? Does this resemble the antagonist of your story? Explain.

CHAPTER TEN

USING DIALOGUE TO MINE YOUR STORY AND TRANSFORM YOUR CHARACTER

Authors and psychotherapists both use dialogue as a means of probing deeper into the human psyche. Through conversation, the threads of an entrenched story can be pulled apart, untangled, and spun into something entirely new. Dialogues, after all, reveal character. They reflect our beliefs, the way we think, our upbringing, and other personal nuances. They can also reveal secrets and our true feelings about relationships, both with ourselves and others. In this regard, they are a great tool for exposing the source of conflicts and identifying the places where resolution can become possible.

In therapy sessions, plays, films, and our everyday human interactions, dialogues are usually spoken between two people. Yet, we experience dialogue inside our heads, too, as various competing internal voices reflect different aspects of ourselves. And while these debates are really monologues, since we are only speaking with ourselves, they tend to have an undeniable conversational quality. That doesn't make us crazy; rather, it makes us human. Naturally and unconsciously, we begin internalizing these voices in early childhood from parents, siblings, teachers, and friends. Think of it this way: a child can only mimic what he hears spoken. Eventually, these internalized voices are assimilated into a template or gestalt of the self. This is why we can often imagine what our parents would say or think if they were speaking to us. If you've ever heard the voice of your mother, your boss, or your therapist in your head, then you understand how powerful such voices can be. It's what we mean when we say someone is impressionable, although it's true for everyone to some degree.

The Omniscient Narrator

This template of voices is larger than the sum of its parts. Moderating all these voices is our inner omniscient narrator, the name I use to describe the quiet still voice that senses the big picture and whispers our truths. When accessed through meditation, prayer, or, for our purposes, through writing, this inner narrator has an uncanny ability to sift through all the competing voices to mine the more expansive, authentic narratives buried in our subconscious. Because it can transcend our baser, egocentric childlike self or any of the internalized critical voices that don't really belong to us, we might also refer to it as the higher self. And because it is omniscient and can access this expanded perspective, it is able to both challenge and understand our undermining voices — so that, even when these voices speak to us, demanding attention, we are no longer ruled by them.

This is, by the way, one reason I insist that clients write in the third-person voice, which is often called the "omniscient narrator." The narrative stance is then distinct from and "above" any particular character's viewpoint. Third-person narration in fiction often, though not always, reflects (or mimics) the perspective of the author, the creator of all the story's characters. When clients adopt this omniscient stance, they see themselves better, and in doing so, sometimes realize that one voice, one internal "character," has actually hijacked their narrative. Because it offers a transcendent lens, one might even consider the third person or omniscient narrator as presenting a spiritual perspective on life.

One way to access our omniscient narrator is to engage it in what it does best — moderating these internal dialogues. That's why, in this chapter's exercises, we will use the literary device of dialogue to access the powerful and expansive voices that can help us overcome our vulnerabilities and embrace our strengths as we delve deeper into the conflict of our chapter narrative.

Talking Back to Our Vulnerabilities

Sometimes our vulnerabilities control our story, leading us to perhaps cower or act aggressively when we feel threatened by an antagonist. We may not be able to make the big move to Paris, ask our boss for a raise, or lose the fifty pounds our doctor says our life depends on because these vulnerabilities are so deeply embedded in our narrative. Perhaps we imagine we'll never survive in a foreign country, or we don't deserve a promotion, or we "can't" lose the weight. Whether or not any of these stories are true, the fear may be very real and overwhelming. How do we keep these narratives from dominating our story? The key is to both notice and talk back to them — to let them know they don't run us.

Most people understand the talking back part. They understand that sometimes you have to challenge your fear and the voices that get you riled up and agitated. Some people have an easier time doing this than others, and if it's hard for you, the dialogue exercises will be especially helpful. However, many people overlook the importance of simply observing their vulnerabilities; rather, they would prefer to skip ahead in the story to the point where the vulnerabilities are overcome, not realizing that it's a process. We can't overcome what we don't understand. Sure, certain moments call for a leap of faith, for swift actions and choices in the face of one's fears. But then contemplation and understanding should follow, and the more you can dispassionately observe how your vulnerabilities work, noticing what motivates them and what strategies they use to dominate, the less power they will have over your story in the long-term.

A word about this latter point: Sometimes, people get discouraged when they can't fully eradicate their vulnerabilities. No matter how hard they try, their vulnerabilities show up, as if on cue, every time a particular antagonist or conflict appears in their narrative. That's often to be expected, and it doesn't mean you're doomed. In her book *Radical Acceptance*,[21] psychotherapist and meditation teacher Tara Brach makes a compelling case that simply acknowledging, or as she puts it, "saying hello," to our vulnerabilities gives them less power. Brach maintains that we often invest tremendous amounts of energy to avoid or root out our vulnerabilities, only to become deflated and discouraged when our best efforts fail. We resist acknowledging our vulnerabilities because we judge them to be bad or wrong. In fact, sometimes vulnerabilities are simply misunderstood or unacknowledged strengths, and they signal our growing edges — if only we would listen to them rather than avoid them. But aside from that — and aside from the fact that our vulnerabilities make us human and can lead to greater intimacy — such judgments only end up making us feel worse. Rather, if we regard an unwelcome vulnerability as, say, an annoying but well-meaning relative whose presence we tolerate when they visit, we'd keep them from getting further under our skin.

When we dialogue with our vulnerabilities through writing, we seek to understand them better so that we can keep them from running our lives, while accessing the more powerful narratives that our inner omniscient narrator illuminates.

Use Your Imagination

Writing these dialogues takes a leap of imagination. In them, you personify attitudes, feelings, and fears in a stream-of-consciousness way; you give these traits a voice and perspective. As such, these exercises require courage, creativity, and a willingness to play. The most constructive dialogues occur when we suspend our egos and our judgments about what is being said and, instead, assume a posture of curiosity and inquisitiveness. What does our omniscient inner narrator have to teach us? Where is there room for growth? What might that look like? Allow yourself to be surprised.

Since this type of internal dialogue is new to many people, I provide some guiding questions below to get your conversation started, along with examples of what these conversations can look like. These are just guidelines; let your own conversations flow in whatever way you imagine. If you want, you can choose to answer the questions directly, without embodying the traits as if they were personalities, but I've found that participants in my workshops get the most out of these exercises when they create dialogues that allow these parts of themselves to talk to one another. People are freer and learn more when they treat this like a conversation.

Finally, these dialogues are one of the few exercises where I invite you to write in the first person, or using "I." Since these are essentially conversations with ourselves, this can feel more natural, and many workshop participants find it easier to "talk" using the first person. Ultimately, for the dialogues, use whatever voice feels right.

Dialoguing with Vulnerabilities Exercise

Review the chart you created for the chapter 9 "Character Vulnerabilities Exercise" (page 113). Select one of the vulnerabilities you identified that relate to the central conflict or the primary antagonist, and craft a dialogue between the protagonist and the vulnerability. Of course, you can do this exercises as many times as you like, and "talk" with as many vulnerabilities as you find helpful, but it's preferable to explore one at a time.

Use the following questions to start or guide your conversation, but feel free to ask other questions that come to you:

1. Where do you come from?
2. Why do you continue to haunt me?
3. What do you want from me?
4. How can I accept your presence with love and compassion without giving you power and control over my life?

Example #1: Fear

PROTAGONIST: Fear, I know you well. Whenever I'm on the brink of making serious changes in my life, you show up to try and convince me of all the things that could go wrong. What do you want from me?

FEAR: I'm just trying to protect you. I don't want you to get hurt.

PROTAGONIST: I appreciate your concern for my well-being, but I need you to cut me some slack so that I can take the steps I need to grow and develop confidence and faith in the process. I may make mistakes, but I will learn from them.

FEAR: But what if you get hurt when you make those mistakes? And what if those mistakes can't be undone? You're not getting any younger. If you listen to me, and stay in your comfort zone, you won't have to face too many uncertainties or feel regret later if you fail to achieve your goals or your dreams.

PROTAGONIST: That's bullshit. Life is full of uncertainty, whether I try new things or stick to my security blanket. Disease, natural disasters — all kinds of things happen that I can't control. As for regrets, what about regretting not trying? What's the point of having a goal or a dream if you're too afraid to put one foot in front of the other? Stop making me second-guess myself. Just leave me alone.

FEAR: But if I don't do my job, and you don't succeed in your efforts, you may fall apart, as you've done before. And then you will question yourself, "Why did I do this?"

PROTAGONIST: Fear, ah, I get it now. You're not trying to hurt me. You care about my safety. However, I think you underestimate me. I'm not the same person I used to be. I've overcome obstacles I never thought I could endure. I'm much stronger, and I value the lessons I've learned from my mistakes, even when they have been painful. So if you must do your job, use some discretion. Show up when I'm about to do something really dumb — like stay up too late when I have an important early-morning meeting or let lust get the best of me. But you're not the boss of me, and I'm stronger than you know.

Example #2: Craving

PROTAGONIST: Craving, why are you so all-consuming sometimes? You follow me around, hounding me every second like a little child — *sugar, sugar, we want sugar.* Why can't you leave me alone for once?

CRAVING: My job is to make you believe that you'll die if you don't give in to me. And I can be very convincing. If you feel empty inside, eat ice cream and you'll feel better. If you're bored, chocolate is always a good pick-me-up. I have mastered the art of temptation. Is it my fault that you're not strong enough to resist?

PROTAGONIST: Stop taunting me. I have the ultimate power, not you. You are a fleeting inclination, a temptress, a trickster who promises immediate gratification only to leave me full of shame and regret. I unmask you, see you for what you are, and let you pass, without succumbing.

CRAVING: Rats, foiled again! I'll get you next time.

PROTAGONIST: Yeah, we'll see about that. I'm cutting carbs. Ha, ha!

Embracing Growing Edges

While you may not always have control over the circumstances of your story, you always have an opportunity to take charge of the narrative by choosing how your ever-evolving protagonist will grow. If every conflict reveals vulnerabilities, it also presents a critical juncture in the character arc, where the protagonist can move in many possible directions depending on his or her goals and attitude. If the protagonist embraces the challenges he or she faces as an invitation to refine aspects of his or her character or to cultivate new strengths, then a positive fate awaits regardless of the outcome of the story, for the protagonist will emerge at least as a better, potentially stronger, and more well-rounded character.

I like to refer to these opportunities as growing edges because they represent the thresholds awaiting new growth. Using the personal training analogy, a man may only be able to bench 150 pounds the first day he joins a gym. But if he wants to develop his biceps, his growing edge would be to "work toward benching 180 pounds." Understanding that reaching this goal takes time, the man would give himself credit each time he lifted weights and exercised the underdeveloped muscle until it became stronger. Similarly, from a narrative perspective, your growing edges describe the areas of your story where there's still a lot of room for improvement, but each day the protagonist pushes forward and stretches the margins. If you kept a workout journal, you could track your character's progression by the number of times he or she did emotional heavy lifting over time. But instead of reps or pounds, the goal would be to cultivate universally accepted character strengths — such as courage, compassion, humility, perseverance, determination, and discipline. As the protagonist of your story, the more emotionally heavy lifting you do, especially in the areas that feel vulnerable, the more power you will have to influence the direction of your narrative.

Let me unpack this further, using some of the terms so far. Regardless of the circumstances, every conflict has a corresponding internal challenge. This is the inner story, and we have the power to influence this story by our interpretation of events and the meaning we give them, which influences our actions. While every conflict reveals vulnerabilities, these conflicts also offer the opportunities to grow in just the ways we need to turn vulnerabilities into strengths. We do so by making a commitment to align our thoughts and actions with the character traits we seek to nurture in ourself. For example, a successful executive who tends to critically judge the less fortunate may, upon losing his job — the antagonist here being unemployment — find himself developing more compassion for himself and others. Similarly, say a middle-aged woman loses her job in a recession. She can't control who hires her, but she can summon the necessary resilience, discipline, resourcefulness, and perseverance to keep trying and find alternate sources of income as necessary. That is the choice facing her: she can either adopt a positive attitude and put forth her best efforts or withdraw and play the victim.

What will she do? The choice she makes will largely be influenced by how conscious she is about her own vulnerabilities and how she tells the story of her unemployment. If she is deeply insecure about her talents and skills — perhaps because they were never seen or appreciated by her parents when she was a child — the woman might interpret the job loss as a reflection of her own unworthiness. If so, her lack of confidence might undermine both her motivation to look for work as well as the impression she makes on prospective employers.

But what if this same woman could see her chapter's latest antagonist — again, unemployment — as providing an opportunity to conquer her historically weak self-esteem — which represents her growing edge — by toning her underdeveloped confidence muscle? If her vulnerability is a tendency to feel insecure, she might address that by assuming the exact opposite posture, that of confidence.

The Yoga of Character Development

What do I mean by *posture*? It's a little like "fake it until you make it." Imagine, for a minute, that adopting a character strength is like committing to a yoga pose (or *asana*). As you assume the pose, your body stretches to embody it, building muscle and becoming stronger. In order to embody the posture of confidence, the unemployed woman might adopt an exercise regimen that includes several daily repetitions of personal affirmations, a diet of supportive relationships, and weekly rounds of therapy to explore her sense of unworthiness. Even if she faces a tough employment market, she can improve her odds of finding a job by working on her internal résumé.

The same approach to conflicts with external obstacles is equally applicable to inner conflicts within oneself. Suppose someone has a tendency to be very argumentative and defensive when others voice different opinions. That person's growing edge would involve overcoming arrogance and assuming a posture of humility. In order to get along better with others, the person would focus on recognizing that there are many valid ways to do things.

Ironically, many times I have observed that once my clients begin to embrace their growing edges, either the antagonist itself or the challenge being presented by the antagonist mysteriously vanishes. It's as if the omnipotent author of our story has, in presenting the conflict, created the perfect foil to help us grow in the direction of our ultimate good.

For example, a soft-spoken client who had trouble being assertive found herself, within the span of a few months, having to deal with two pushy antagonists, a coworker and a roommate, whose disrespectful behaviors were upsetting her. She had grown up with a father whose temper made her feel that standing up for herself was unsafe. Framing her antagonists as personal trainers for her personal development helped her muster the courage to set boundaries and express her needs with each of these individuals, which she did in a very ethical and respectful manner. Oddly enough, after she did so, her roommate moved out and her coworker resigned. My client remarked that it seemed strange that her antagonists disappeared once she learned her lesson, as if they were no longer needed.

Her experience suggests an inherent value in simply being able to reframe the way we perceive problems and then to respond with personal integrity. Understanding that our antagonist has something valuable to teach us can help us release our victim mentality and mine the gems of any situation, whether or not our story unfolds to our liking. Suddenly, responding to conflict with anger and resentment or with introspection and empowerment becomes a conscious choice. This new awareness can transform our personal narratives into paeans to the triumph of the human spirit over adversity, reminding us that character development is at the heart of any story worth reading, and also worth living.

The Rent Comes Due: Olivia's Story

I once had a twenty-five-year-old client, Olivia, who wrestled with anger issues. Olivia often butted heads with her roommate, who was a recurrent antagonist in her story, and she had a tendency to spend beyond her means. One month, Olivia's bimonthly paycheck was late due to an administrative error, and she was unable to make her rent. Rather than explain the situation to her roommate, Olivia avoided her roommate entirely.

When her roommate sent her an email asking to have a conversation about the rent that evening, Olivia immediately started rehearsing her defense in her head. She had always paid her rent on time before. Why couldn't her roommate cut her a little slack? After all, Olivia hadn't freaked out when her roommate's cat had peed on her faux bearskin rug. By the time she got to my office that afternoon, Olivia was fuming.

Olivia decided to do the antagonist and vulnerability writing exercises (from chapters 8, 9, and 10) to understand her reaction and figure out next steps. She identified her roommate as her antagonist, and then she identified the obstacle causing conflict, the vulnerability being exposed, and the growing edge she could cultivate by successfully navigating the conflict. Olivia came to see that her inability to pay rent was exposing a tendency to be defensive, conflict avoidant, and extravagant.

But the situation also presented her with an opportunity to cultivate financial and personal responsibility. Olivia recognized that her own concerns about money had nothing to do with her roommate's curiosity about the late rent. When they met later that evening, Olivia was surprised to see how calm she felt as she listened to her roommate's concerns and as she took responsibility for her role in creating the conflict.

Dialoguing with Growing Edges Exercise

In this exercise, you add to the chart you've been developing in chapters 8 and 9. Then, you again create a dialogue, this time between the protagonist and the growing edge that relates to the primary antagonist and vulnerability.

First, add a column on the right side of the chart entitled "Growing Edges." Following the example below, identify and name the character strengths that are being presented by the vulnerability. There may be more than one, and you can name a strength or use a descriptive phrase. For inspiration, refer to the chapter 9 list of character strengths (see page 109), or feel free to characterize the opportunity for growth more loosely, such as "to stand up for myself," "to be a better listener," or "to allow things to unfold naturally." As before, there are no right or wrong answers. The pairing of vulnerabilities and growing edges in the chart below are just examples; change or revise these pairings to fit your circumstances and story.

Conflict	Antagonist	Vulnerabilities	Growing Edges
Planning a wedding	Mom	Desire for approval Lack of self-trust Fear of independence Conflicting loyalties	Assertiveness Independence Sensitivity Compromise
Unemployment	Bad economy/competitive job market	Impatience Easily discouraged Exhaustion Fear of failure Self-doubt	Perseverance Faith Confidence
Empty nest	The protagonist	Loneliness Fear of growing old Self-doubt Lack of direction Shame	To embrace uncertainty Rediscovery and reinvention
Divorce	Soon-to-be ex-spouse	Anger Resentment Fear of being alone Guilt Embarrassment	Forgiving my ex Forgiving myself Independence Acceptance Assertiveness

Once you have filled in the chart, craft a dialogue between the protagonist and a growing edge that relates to the primary antagonist and vulnerability. If you used a phrase to describe your growing edge — for example, "to embrace uncertainty" — try to replace this with a word, preferably a character strength, that encapsulates the same meaning — perhaps "peace" or "contentment." This makes the growing edge easier to personify. Once again, you may write the dialogue in the first-person voice (using "I"), if that's more natural. Here are some questions to start or guide you conversation:

1. How can I access more of you?
2. What gets in the way of making you a bigger part of my life?
3. Where are you hiding, and how do I get you to come out and play?

Example #1: Courage

PROTAGONIST: Courage, how can I access more of you?

COURAGE: First, know that I'm inside you — have always been there, since you took your first little baby steps.

PROTAGONIST: But why do I have trouble finding you?

COURAGE: Fear made you think that I had gone away. But I lay nestled like a lion under your security blanket, waiting for you to pull the covers off and exclaim, "Let's go, it's time to take a stroll through the jungle."

PROTAGONIST: Ha, ha. You have a great sense of humor, Courage. Wish I could find the humor when I'm in my fearful place. Life seems so serious then, like every choice I make has monstrous consequences.

COURAGE: The monster is not the consequence; the monster is the fear.

PROTAGONIST: Yes, but it feels so big.

COURAGE: So shrink it down and put it in its proper place. If you can be slightly more courageous than you are afraid, you'll be in good shape. Trust me, I know what I'm doing.

Example #2: Self-Compassion

PROTAGONIST: Self-compassion, how can I access more of you? I'm always beating myself up for not being good enough.

SELF-COMPASSION: You're not really seeing yourself clearly, and you're diminishing all your strengths and good qualities. No one is judging you the way you're judging yourself. If you want to access more of me, the first thing you need to do is put down the weapons you use against yourself — criticism, doubt, and jealousy.

PROTAGONIST: I've carried around these weapons for what seems like my entire life. I feel like they're part of me. I wouldn't even know how to put them down. And quite honestly, I'm not sure that I want to get rid of them. Sometimes they motivate me to do more and be more.

SELF-COMPASSION: You're under the mistaken impression that you need to change something about yourself to feel worthy or lovable. All you really need to do is make a commitment to love yourself unconditionally, flaws and all. After all, you're human. Once you have unconditional self-love, your best self will just show up naturally.

Example #3: Willpower

PROTAGONIST: Willpower, how can I access more of you? I know you're inside me, but it's hard to reach you when I need you, especially when I'm being tempted by cravings for sweets. How do I access you?

WILLPOWER: First, you need to slow down and become aware of when you are being tempted, and then ask yourself about the consequences of your actions. If the negative consequences outweigh the benefits, you will find me easier to access. It all depends on how much you really want to lose weight.

CHAPTER ELEVEN

SUPPORTING CHARACTERS AND OTHER RESOURCES

In the wake of my father's death, I lost lots of sleep worrying about how I would manage his affairs, which entailed wading through complicated financials, including stocks and bonds I knew nothing about, and selling a house, which I had never done before.

Lost, exhausted, and at an emotional ebb, I looked to my father's bookshelf for distraction. What I found instead was inspiration — a copy of *The Hero with a Thousand Faces*. Written by the great cultural anthropologist Joseph Campbell, this work of nonfiction describes the hero's journey, a story featuring certain common themes that has been told around tables and campfires in every language and in every culture since ancient times. According to Campbell, in classic myth, the strength of the kingdom reflected the health of the king and queen. When the rulers were not well, either figuratively or literally, the kingdom became a wasteland, prompting the hero to take a quest, find a sacred object, and return home to heal the land.[22] While it has many variations, the hero's journey has a simple core plot: the hero hears a call to leave home, sets out on a journey, faces all kind of obstacles and demons, redeems a treasure, and returns home victorious and enriched, thereby saving the "kingdom."

Sound familiar? You might recognize permutations of this journey from classic stories and myths like *The Odyssey*, the Fisher King parable, the biblical story of Jacob, and even *The Wizard of Oz*. As a psychotherapist, I have always been intrigued by Swiss psychologist Carl Jung's take on the hero's journey as a story about spiritual transformation.

What struck me most, during my restless night, was Campbell's point that every hero is given the necessary preparation, tools, and support to fulfill his or her quest. The hero is either bestowed with swords to fight dragons, magical powers to fight demons, or superhuman strengths to fight superbad guys, and characters always appear to offer the hero support and guidance along the way.

By identifying with the hero, we aren't meant to imagine ourselves as heroes in any mythological sense. But we are all certainly on a journey and in need of both reassurance and inspiration. Nobody is going to rescue us. Instead, we need to access our own inner superhero to save our inner selves.

I took all this to heart as I thought about the journey I was now on after my father's death. I pondered the following questions, allowing my responses to arise naturally (and framing them in the third-person narrative):

- *What is the conflict of this chapter?* My response: Managing her father's estate while grieving and recovering from an intense period of caregiving.
- *What strengths does the hero of this story possess to aid*

in accomplishing this task? My response: Intelligence, resourcefulness, resilience, and discipline; she knows to get to the gym when stress levels peak, and she has the humility to ask questions if she doesn't understand something.

- *What is the vulnerability being revealed?* My response: She has the financial acumen of a twelfth grader, is disorganized and emotionally exhausted, and has a tendency to become easily frustrated when things don't go as expected.

- *What is this experience testing? What is the growing edge?* My response: This is a test of endurance, courage, discipline, and flexibility.

- *What tools and resources has she been given to help her?* My response: Computer skills, a healthy body, a gym, a flexible schedule, financial resources, written instructions from her father, and contact numbers at different financial institutions.

- *Who are her supporting characters?* My response: A ton of loving friends and relatives, some of whom have expertise in financial matters and real estate; they will root for her and, if needed, offer advice.

- *What evidence does she have that she can manage these responsibilities?* My response: She's often been thrust into jobs and situations where she had to improvise, drawing on her knowledge, wits, and ability to ask thoughtful questions. Each time, she has risen to the challenge, defying other's expectations and her own.

I put down my pen and realized the tension in my chest had subsided. Subsequently, whenever I became stressed, I referred back to this journal entry for reassurance. When I felt discouraged, I reminded myself of my talents and skills. When I got confused, I turned to my resources for information, support, and relief. Eventually, everything got done because I was able to marshal all the gifts at my disposal.

If facing the conflict in your story seems scary or overwhelming, you can exercise your heroic powers in two ways. First, you can take charge of your story by doing what you've done thus far — reframing the situation as an opportunity to strengthen your character. The nature of this work is internal, meaning you don't need to take any actions or change anything in your outer story to change the way you feel about your story. However, remember that, as the hero of your own story, you always have strengths and resources. You can also examine how to marshal the collective benevolent forces outside of yourself to give you additional support.

After all, you wouldn't attempt to climb Mount Everest without taking stock of your physical and mental fitness, nor would you take an important test without assessing what you know and identifying the areas that need improvement. In a similar vein, when an antagonist in a story presents you with challenges, prepare to tackle them by becoming consciously aware of your capabilities, your vulnerabilities, your goals for improvement, and all the people, resources, practices, inspirations, and lessons learned from previous life experiences that support you.

The conflict of your story is yours alone to face — no one can develop those character muscles for you. Yet you can turn to your supporting characters and other resources for moral support, information, inspiration, and practical help. In fact, in ancient and contemporary stories, one of the most important lessons the hero must learn is how to gather and use all the people, resources, and special tools (such as Dorothy's ruby slippers) already at his or her disposal. The hero must also learn the lessons from previous chapters to help steer through the current uncharted or treacherous waters. After all, why place characters in difficult situations without equipping them with the resources they need to successfully navigate them?

You may not realize the full strength of the collective forces in your favor until you take an inventory of them, which is what we're going to do in this chapter.

Supporting Characters: Fairy Godmothers and Sidekicks

Behind every protagonist, supporting characters provide love, support, and encouragement on the journey. They are the fairy godmothers and sidekicks who keep the protagonist on course and moving forward in a positive direction. Often these supporting characters are heroes and heroines in their own right. When the protagonist confronts the antagonist, these characters offer words of wisdom at just the right time, or they come to the hero's rescue at just the right moment. Where would Dorothy be without Scarecrow, Lion, and the Tin Man? Harry Potter without Hermione and Ron?

In stories, the key is that the hero must identify these helpers and ask for help. Assistance must be requested or it often doesn't come. In your life, you probably have a good idea of who the supporting characters of your story are. They may be spouses, children, friends, teachers, relatives, and mentors. They may be teammates, colleagues, clergy, therapists, and pets. They may be members of your family, social network, community, or religion. Some consider the Divine or a higher power to be the ultimate supporting character.

Who among these could you ask for help, and what help

might they provide in your story? Supporting characters generally do some or all of the following:

- Love you unconditionally
- Expand your own capacity to love and connect
- Mirror back to you what is good about yourself
- Accept and forgive your shortcomings
- Display a continuing commitment to your well-being
- Offer perspectives beyond your familiar way of seeing things
- Comfort you emotionally and physically
- Support you when you are struggling to care for yourself
- Listen to you when you need to talk
- Offer constructive feedback when appropriate and necessary
- Appreciate your gifts
- Share and/or support your goals
- Make you feel safe enough to feel vulnerable
- Challenge you to expand yourself emotionally and spiritually
- Lend practical help when you need a hand, perhaps babysitting, fixing your car, or lending you money

Even simply bringing your supporting characters to mind can be beneficial during the darker chapters of your story. Case in point: When a client of mine was going through a very difficult custody battle, she made a point of meditating each morning and picturing the faces of all the people in her life who were "on her team," so to speak. Thinking about her parents, her brother, her children, and her friends helped anchor her as she faced animosity from her ex-husband and his lawyer.

While it may be true that love conquers all, your supporting characters can certainly give you that extra oomph to conquer whatever challenges present themselves in the conflict of your narrative.

Supporting Characters Exercise

Please answer the following questions in the third-person narrative.

1. Generally speaking, who are the protagonist's supporting characters? How does each of these characters already offer support?

2. Picture a scene in which the protagonist faces the antagonist. Which supporting characters would you write into the scene, and what would they say or do to help? If you feel inspired, write the scene as a story narrative, or as a dialogue you'd find in a play or film.

3. What steps might the protagonist take to get more support from his or her supporting characters? How might the protagonist request more or better support?

4. Imagine reframing the antagonist as a supporting character (or supporting circumstance). How might the antagonist actually be helping the protagonist become a better person?

Tools and Resources

Perhaps you recall reading a book or watching a film where the hero — in the very throes of danger and about to die — suddenly remembers a weapon or some magical object that saves the day. How could the hero have forgotten? Yet in life as in literature, when under stress, we often overlook all the resources at our disposal even when they are staring us in the face. Tools and resources are tangible things, systems, and organizations that you can leverage to successfully help you overcome obstacles in your narrative. Obvious examples include money, professional associations, a gym membership, and personal possessions like a car or a house that we might take for granted. Some less obvious resources are sentimental objects like photo albums or old letters from loved ones that you can turn to for emotional succor in difficult moments. Did you lose your job? Well, your house could serve as your temporary office, and your car as a way to get to interviews or start your bagel delivery business. Did you go to college? Well, you might consider accessing the alumni career services of your alma mater. Are you overeating to cope with stress? Start using that gym membership you purchased at the beginning of the year.

Often, a protagonist's ability to marshal his or her strengths is what's necessary to use tools and resources wisely, so they become blessings and not burdens. For example, Dorothy's accidental acquisition of the ruby slippers puts her in danger, but they are necessary and she can't simply get rid of them. On the contrary, she must cultivate her strengths on her journey through Oz — courage, loving-kindness, clarity, and appreciation for the life she ran away from in Kansas — in order to access the slippers' power to return home.

The same idea holds true in real life. A gym membership simply drains your wallet if you don't muster the discipline to use it. If your power tools lay rusting in a storage bin in the attic, they won't work when you need them, and then what's the point of keeping them in the first place?

Sometimes, we may find resources in unlikely places. For example, a financially challenged client of mine realized she could pawn her very expensive wedding ring to help pay for her divorce. This action not only alleviated some of her financial worries but felt symbolically transformative.

Even if we're not ready or sure how to use our resources, taking inventory is the first step toward understanding how to best leverage our assets. Once we can see what we're working with, we can make informed choices about how best to move forward, seeking assistance when and if necessary.

Resource Assessment Exercise

Answer the following questions in the third-person narrative.

1. What are the protagonist's resources? Explain.
2. How might the protagonist marshal his or her personal strengths (for example, courage, intelligence, and creativity) to best utilize these resources to navigate the conflict in the current chapter?
3. If the protagonist is not ready to utilize certain resources, how might the protagonist prepare to be ready?
4. What are the consequences if the protagonist fails to leverage these resources?

Inspirational Motifs and Mantras

Thinking about inspirational people, ideas, and symbols can also guide you through difficult chapters in your life. I like to call these "motifs and mantras." A motif is a symbolic object or image that represents ideas, beliefs, and emotions. For example, hearts remind us of love, while birds might remind us of freedom or transcendence. Stars are common symbols in many countries and religions, representing specific people's beliefs and histories. Animals, constellations, and nature provide many common symbols.

Although your first reaction to a challenge may not be to conjure an inspirational image, perhaps you have a good luck charm, meaningful pieces of jewelry, wall art, or even tattoos that comfort or inspire you, or perhaps remind you of who you are, what you're capable of, or who you aspire to be.

Because they are both subjective and deeply personal, symbols can carry us even through the most trying of times. One of my clients involved in a difficult divorce wore a gold lighthouse pinned to the lapel of her coat to remind her that her journey through dark, rough seas would eventually come to an end and that she would find her way to shore.

Similarly, metaphors or analogies can also anchor us in specific frames of mind when experiencing intense periods of personal growth. A successful professional returning to work after a heart attack used the concept of a .300 batting average — that a baseball player who gets a hit three out of every ten at-bats is considered excellent by major league standards — as a framework for putting less pressure on himself and his colleagues to do everything flawlessly all the time. To reinforce this metaphor, he posted a baseball card by his desk with a note that read ".300."

Mantras, too, can also be extremely helpful. Originating in the Hindu and Buddhist traditions, and now popularized through yoga and meditation, mantras are essentially words of wisdom or spiritual ideas that we can repeat, out loud or in our minds, over and over again to manage anxiety, combat depression, or just simply maintain peace of mind. Examples of mantras include "Om," "Let go, let God," or perhaps "Feelings aren't facts."

Last but not least, prayers — whether or not they are part of a formal religious or spiritual practice — are also very powerful tools for navigating transition. By articulating our hopes, fears, and desires, and calling on a higher power for assistance, we may find the inner strength to stretch ourselves in ways we might never have imagined.

Motifs and Metaphors Exercise

Answer the following questions in the third-person narrative.

1. What motifs and metaphors can the protagonist turn to for support, hope, and inspiration? Explain.

2. In what tangible ways might he or she bring these motifs and metaphors to mind when needed? For example, could the protagonist get a tattoo or post something on the refrigerator?

3. What mantras or prayers might help the protagonist address the challenges presented by the antagonist in the chapter?

4. Imagine you've been asked to provide illustrations to go along with the story about the current chapter of your life. What images or symbols would you suggest? Explain why you chose them. If inspired, design an image or symbol that represents what this chapter means to you, and consider displaying this image or symbol in some way, as a reminder when you need it.

Lessons Learned from Previous Chapters

Finally, we often possess the wisdom from previous chapters of our story, which can help guide us in steering through the current conflict. While there's a first time for everything, the older we get, the more we accumulate knowledge and confidence from prior experiences that we can draw upon when we find ourselves in new and potentially challenging territory.

Perhaps we have skills that helped us in a previous situation that can be easily transferred to the task at hand. Even just a vague sense that "I've felt this way before and somehow managed to survive" can remind us of our own competencies and resilience.

For example, when challenged with managing my father's estate, I had to remind myself that I had often been thrust into overwhelming situations, where, lacking the necessary experience, I had to improvise, drawing on my innate talents and strengths. Somehow, this has been the story of my career. For instance, at the age of twenty-three, my first job was as the editor of a weekly community newspaper, where I had to write three stories a week, manage a reporter, edit articles and columns, write headlines, lay out the paper manually (before computer pagination), interact with the public, and write endorsements of politicians. I successfully managed that crazy job for five years before burning out toward the end. By contrast, I was now older and wiser, and while I would be undertaking the responsibilities of my father's estate while grieving, it would only last a year.

Learned Lessons Exercise

Please answer the following questions in the third-person narrative.

1. What evidence does the protagonist have that he or she is up to this challenge? Has the protagonist handled something similar before? If so, what helped? If inspired, write the story of these earlier experiences in the third-person narrative.

2. Write a third-person narrative that describes how the protagonist applies the lessons of the past to surmount the challenges presented by her current antagonist.

CHAPTER TWELVE

CLIMAX: AS YOUR STORY TURNS

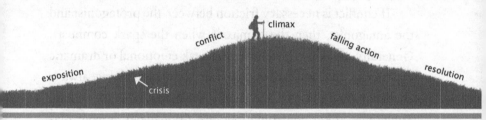

> *When a resolute young fellow steps up to the great bully, the world, and takes him boldly by the beard, he is often surprised to find it comes off in his hand, and that it was only tied on to scare away the timid adventurers.*
>
> — Ralph Waldo Emerson, quoted in
> *Dictionary of Proverbs* edited by Grenville Kleiser

Climax: The highest, most intense point in a story in which the conflict between the protagonist and antagonist comes to a head.

Thus far, your protagonist has marshaled strengths and resources, received help from supporting characters, raised his or her banner, reflected on the wisdom gleaned from previous experiences, and made peace with his or her vulnerabilities, transforming them to assets where possible. The protagonist is now ready for the climax, the turning point of the story when the main character confronts the primary antagonist and any other obstacles that have stood in his or her path. By definition, the climax is the point of no return where the protagonist must continue on his or her current course of action because turning back is physically or emotionally impossible in some way.

If conflict is necessary friction between the protagonist and the antagonist, then the climax is when the spark combusts. Generally speaking, the climax is a peak emotional or dramatic experience. In classic adventure stories, the hero almost always challenges and destroys the enemy, the monster, or the villain. Sometimes these confrontations are dramatized as epic dialogues where the hero takes a stand against a bad guy or the forces of evil — such as in *Star Wars* when Luke Skywalker declares, "I'll never turn to the dark side."

Of course, in real life, climactic confrontations don't involve the destruction of others but confronting and slaying one's inner dragons to achieve an important outer goal. And yet, here too this can mean engaging one's antagonist in constructive dialogue and/or standing your ground. Perhaps your protagonist finally musters the courage to confront a bully, come out of the closet, profess romantic feelings for a best friend, or ask for a divorce. Or perhaps the protagonist undertakes some consequential actions, like closing on a house or landing a new job, that change the outer story, or his or her circumstances.

The climax in novels and films is easy to identify: it comes at the end. But in real life, we usually can't predict how our story will unfold or identify in the moment what event might prove to be the climax, especially when we're focusing on our current chapter. After all, this is your own story you're creating, and the ending isn't written yet. Still, after a period of mounting suspense or tension, you may have a sense that an important conversation needs to happen, an action must be taken, or a decision must be made, one you may have been postponing. That's why, in the next series of exercises, I want you to begin to envision what the climax of your chapter might look like, setting a positive intention for what you wish to happen while letting go of expectations. This can be a helpful mind-set to embrace in any challenging, unpredictable situation.

Envisioning the best possible climax can help you strategize how you might achieve your desired resolution — for example, preparing yourself properly to take an important test or facing a judge about a custody settlement. It can also prompt you to get emotionally and physically ready, such as when expectant mothers take pregnancy and Lamaze classes. Many athletes practice positive visualization: a figure skater pursuing an Olympic gold medal will imagine performing a triple Axel perfectly, which may help him or her execute it well when performing.

Thinking about the climax — what it may entail and what result you'd like — may also help you sort through conflicting thoughts and feelings. For example, if you're planning to have an oft-postponed "big talk" with a significant other about your relationship, it helps to "get your story straight" — in other words, to plan for the best moment to talk and to consider carefully what you want to say.

Identifying the Climax

Perhaps you have a clear idea of what your climax might look like, or perhaps you have only a vague sense that something inevitable needs to be done. But if you're still not sure, think of the climax of your narrative as the pinnacle of your character development arc in the present moment — the point when you do the thing you most need to do to get unstuck so you can move to the next chapter of your story. It may be the moment when confidence conquers doubt, courage overcomes fear, or persistence overcomes resistance, prompting you to take some seemingly inevitable action that changes your story. As you consider what this could be, check in with your intuition and your feelings; they usually signal when that opportunity you've been waiting for, or perhaps dreading, is just around the corner. You may, for example, begin to feel a pressure-cooker-like atmosphere — perhaps a mix of excitement, anxiety, or a little of both. Close your eyes and follow the trajectory of feelings as if they were a footpath leading to a scenic outlook offering a bird's-eye view of your narrative. Pay attention to the thoughts and images that emerge. Perhaps there is an epiphany just within reach, a sure sign that you're nearing the climax.

In fact, epiphanies often immediately precede or accompany the climax of the story. That's because the actualization of the protagonist's character arc elicits important realizations, which crown the hero's transformation. Luke realizes he'll never turn to the dark side, and says so out loud, striking a chord that prompts Darth Vader to save him. Typically, we can't rush epiphanies; they come in their own time, when we're ready. Still, just beginning to imagine what possible insights our protagonist might have can help us shed light on our current circumstances so we can find our way forward.

Finally, we live in a world where crystal balls are as fallible as foresight, so it's important to remain open to the unexpected.

Sometimes, we anticipate how events will transpire as a way to protect ourselves. We imagine the worst possible scenario to avoid disappointment, or we build up our defenses in preparation for a fight. Such mental games can create undue anxiety and work against us. But who knows how things will turn out? While envisioning the climax can help you get emotionally, physically, and mentally prepared, keep in mind that life often surprises us, in both good and not-so-good ways. What if, after preparing for battle, your antagonist surprises you by baring his or her soul, expressing deep remorse for his or her part in your troubles? Keeping your dukes raised will only result in hurting yourself. That's why, when preparing for the climax, it's always good to keep an open mind and an equally open heart.

Writing Your Peak Climax Exercise

Now it's time to explore the climax of your narrative.

Imagine you're reading the story of your life, and you've come to the current chapter. Review some or all of the writing you've done so far, in which you've explored the primary conflict, the primary antagonist, your own strengths and vulnerabilities, your resources; remember and understand all the forces at work and what's at stake. The antagonist has been pushing you to stretch and strengthen yourself in some way, so how will you respond? The tension has built and the moment of truth has arrived. What would an ideal climax look like?

In story form, using the third-person narrative, write that scene in as much detail as possible, describing your desired outcome. Consider some or all of the following as guidelines:

1. What are the protagonist's hopes and fears in regard to the primary antagonist?

2. How might the protagonist act in a way that would cultivate his or her desired character strengths and growing edges (as identified in chapters 9 and 10)?

3. How might he or she marshal strengths, resources, and supporting characters to achieve this (as identified in chapter 11)?

4. Imagine the hero has an epiphany. What might this look like?

When you've completed this narrative of the ideal climax, write a second version also in story form. In this one, consider what the protagonist might be willing to let go of if things don't go as planned. What might the protagonist do, say, or think to take care of him- or herself? In what ways can the protagonist act to cultivate his or her desired character strengths and growing edges even if the climax does not play out in an ideal way?

Finally, consider how you could prepare for the climaxes you envision. What action steps might you take to feel as mentally, emotionally, and physically prepared as possible? Then, visualize the climaxes you've written; see them play out in your mind's eye.

Once you've done this, let them go and allow the actual climax in your life to unfold naturally, in whatever way is appropriate, trusting that you have done everything in your power to manifest your vision.

Envisioning the Climax: Lisa's Breakup

Lisa was a sunny, brilliant twenty-four-year-old New Yorker who sought counseling to resolve a relationship crisis. She had been with her live-in boyfriend Alex since she was eighteen — he was the only lover she had ever known. Although they were best friends, their sex life had fizzled, and she found herself restless and interested in other men. She longed to travel, to explore new lifestyles and places, and yet her boyfriend had familial and professional roots in Manhattan.

Then Lisa was offered a great new job at a large, reputable company in Seattle; it was an opportunity that could launch her career. So Lisa decided it was time to end the relationship. She accepted the job (which didn't start for another month), and yet she was experiencing anxiety in anticipation of the breakup. She worried about hurting Alex and that she might never find a man who was as loyal and devoted.

When I asked her to envision the climax of her current chapter, Lisa wrote the following:

Lisa makes plans with Alex to spend Saturday afternoon in Central Park. The night before, she writes a long letter to Alex, not sure if she'll send or read it to him, to express all of her thoughts and feelings about the relationship. She does this to make sure her head and her heart are clear, so that she says the right things. Saturday morning, she goes to yoga, which helps her feel more relaxed and centered. She doesn't want to start bawling uncontrollably when she tells him she's moving, but perhaps it can't be helped. She meets Alex at their usual spot at Sheep Meadow. She brings him his favorite organic turkey sandwich. He can tell something is up — he always can read her so well, which is one of the reasons she loves him.

She takes a deep breath and tells him she got offered the Seattle job. He looks scared but forces a smile. He says, "Congratulations. I knew you'd get it. They'd be stupid not to hire you." She starts crying — it couldn't be helped. He hugs her. She tells him she loves him, that he is the greatest

*boyfriend anyone could ever want. She explains how she
has been agonizing about what to do, that she wants to go,
and that she thinks it's best if they break up. She notices
tears in his eyes and feels terrible. But he listens to her and
gives her a big hug. He tells her he loves her, too, and that
he doesn't want to her to leave, but that he can't stop her. He
acknowledges that she hasn't seemed happy lately, and yet
he has felt powerless to do anything to help her. He understands their relationship has been more like a friendship
lately, and maybe he also has thoughts about other women.
They hug each other even harder, both understanding what
must be done, even if it hurts, which it will. But she also
knows they will both be okay...and who knows, in five or
ten years, if they are both still single, and it's meant to
be...they will find each other again.*

Upon completing the exercise, Lisa reflected on how she
would take care of herself if her breakup with Alex didn't go as
well as she hoped.

*She sits alone, weeping, on a picnic blanket at Sheep
Meadow. The turkey sandwich is still neatly wrapped in
plastic, untouched. Alex stormed off shortly after she broke
the news. He was angry and said some pretty horrible
things. Lisa knows that Alex didn't really mean all those
things — he was just hurt. Still, it was hard to see him so
distraught and know that she was to blame. She comforts
herself by reminding herself that she never meant to hurt
him, and that hiding the truth of her feelings would only
cause them both more heartbreak in the long run. She tells*

herself that it took courage to be honest. Still, she worries what will happen when she goes home. Having planned for the contingency that Alex would be upset, she decides to take up Rachel's invitation to stay at her place. This will be good for her because she could use the emotional support. She knows Alex well enough to understand he'll need some time, and she trusts that he will come around. Even if he hates her for the rest of her life, which she thinks is unlikely, she knows she did the right thing. As the first of many waves of sadness begin to wash over her, she tells herself, "This too shall pass."

In the end, Lisa's conversation with Alex played out somewhere between her ideal and her less-than-ideal scenario, as is true of many real-life climaxes. Alex took the news well at first, but then he got very angry with her the next day, prompting Lisa to sleep on Rachel's couch for a few days to weather the storm. Eventually, Lisa moved back in and proceeded to prepare herself for the move to Seattle with Alex's ambivalent support. Like most stories, there were some loose ends that still needed tying, but at least the cat was out of the bag (and in chapter 13, we'll learn how Lisa's story ultimately resolved).

Lisa's story raises an important question: How can you feel good about the climax of your narrative when so many influential factors are beyond your control? Can you make peace with your antagonist even if your antagonist refuses to make peace with you? Yes, you can, if you're willing to engage in a productive dialogue with the antagonistic voices in your mind.

Dialoguing with Your Antagonist

Even if you can't predict the climax of your story, feeling ready to step up to the challenges presented by the narrative conflict is often half, if not the entire, battle. After all, before you can conquer your antagonist, you need to conquer whatever vulnerabilities — including fears, doubts, resentments, or misgivings — are preventing you from progressing to the next chapter of your narrative. Some internal struggle typically precedes the resolution of any conflict. What if you felt so mentally, physically, and emotionally ready to face the challenges ahead that your sense of confidence and empowerment was success enough — so that you wouldn't have to even "win" the battle? Metaphorically speaking, what if you could ask your antagonist for a blessing, knowing you deserved one, without it mattering whether or not you received it? This would be a beautiful climax indeed.

One of my favorite examples of this comes from the Bible, and it's so rich in meaning that you don't need to be religiously or spiritually inclined to appreciate the symbolism or the message. The book of Genesis tells the story of Jacob, who pretends to be his brother, Esau, so he can steal his family's birthright. One interpretation is that Jacob must resort to deception because he doesn't have the courage to ask his father for a blessing outright. Fearing his brother will retaliate, Jacob runs away from home. Many years later, when Jacob has his own family, he hears that Esau is approaching. Fearing for his life and those he loves, Jacob divides his family into two camps, surmising that if Esau kills half his family, at least the other half will survive. But Jacob changes his mind and realizes that he must face his antagonist by himself. Representing the climax of this particular narrative, Jacob wrestles all night with a "stranger," which some sources identify as an angel. When the stranger realizes he cannot win, he dislocates Jacob's hip socket, wounding him. Yet Jacob refuses to give up, insisting that the stranger bless him. Recognizing that Jacob is no longer the child who, fearing rejection, couldn't ask for what he wanted, the angel not only blesses him but changes his name to "Israel," the angel says, "because you have become great before God and won."[23] This name change crowns Jacob's metamorphosis. Later, when Jacob reunites with his brother, Esau, they embrace, their conflict resolved.

This parable offers many meaningful lessons about climaxes. For starters, receiving a blessing from our antagonist at the climax of our story can be transformative. The conferring of a blessing suggests that the conflict has been resolved, peace restored, and all our struggles have been worthwhile. Especially if our antagonist is a person, we may hope that he or she will come to understand our position or validate our choices, so that we might achieve a sense of closure. But in order to secure the blessing, it helps if we can give it to ourself first. After all, you can't ask for something you don't think you've earned or even deserve. If you're not there already, you can begin by wrestling with the voices of the antagonist that inhabit your mind.

In fact, even if you can't secure your antagonist's blessing, you can still successfully resolve the conflict of your story by challenging these conflicting voices. One might even argue that Jacob didn't really need the angel's blessing because he "won" the moment he conquered his fears and doubts by asking for what he wanted, embracing his growing edge of "assertiveness." A client of mine put it this way, "I used to think about how I might have the perfect conversation with my mother so that she could really understand me. I thought if she understood me, I'd finally have her approval, and then I'd feel like I was okay. Eventually, I realized that it didn't matter what words I chose, or how perfectly I expressed myself, because her own issues were preventing her from really hearing me. I knew that if I could quiet the voice in my head that tells me I'm difficult, even if this voice could be traced back to my mother, I would no longer need her approval, and this, in itself, would feel like a victory."

Another lesson of the Jacob narrative, and one suggested in my client's confessional, is that we are all on our own unique, individual inner journeys. While we may lean on the love and encouragement of our supporting characters, and share with them the fruit of our labors, in the moment of truth, the climax of our conflict with our antagonist is ours alone to face. In the spirit of this individual journey, I invite you to complete the next exercise, a dialogue with your inner antagonist.

Dialoguing with Your Antagonist Exercise

Often, when we anticipate a difficult confrontation, we imagine arguments with people that bear little resemblance to real conversations, and we mostly imagine how we will defend and justify our position. To avoid this unproductive mental exercise, please follow the instructions to this exercise very carefully. Consider the prompts as guardrails that keep you from straying into negativity.

Imagine that you've been asked to interview your antagonist for an article you're writing entitled "Antagonists Make the Best Teachers." The antagonist has appeared in this chapter to teach you something you didn't know about yourself, and your job is to explore what that is. Imagine that your antagonist has taken a truth serum that forces him or her to be completely candid and atypically self-aware. Follow the writing prompts below in precisely the order they are presented. If you feel the desire to add questions of your own, do so, but be sure to maintain the same spirit of openness and curiosity, lest this dialogue degenerate into an unwinnable argument. For this exercise, as with the dialogue exercises in chapters 9 and 10, I recommend using the first-person ("I") voice. Treat this like a direct conversation.

1. What brings you into my life right now?
2. What motivates you to do what you do?
3. What are you trying to teach me?
4. How can I learn to live with you?
5. How might I learn to live without you?

When you've completed this short dialogue, thank the antagonist for sharing, and then proceed to give your protagonist the blessing he or she is seeking from the antagonist. This blessing can be as brief or as long as you need it to be (see an example below). When you've finished, reflect on what it felt like to bless yourself.

Example: The Bully

PROTAGONIST [MONICA]: What brings you into my life now?

ANTAGONIST: Your author has placed me in your story to bully you until you have no other choice but to stand up for and take care of yourself.

PROTAGONIST: What motivates you to do what you do?

ANTAGONIST: It's nothing personal. Bullying is the only way I know how to have personal power and control. It's how I survived growing up in my family. Now I just do what I do because it's the only way I know how to get what I want. I don't know any other way.

PROTAGONIST: What are you trying to teach me?

ANTAGONIST: I'm trying to teach you not to take things so personally and to stand up for yourself so I don't get under your skin.

PROTAGONIST: How can I learn to live with you?

ANTAGONIST: That choice is yours. You can learn to live with me by doing things and surrounding yourself with people that make you feel strong so that my criticisms are a reflection of me, which they are. That way, when I say something bullying, even if you feel a sting, it will only last for a brief second and you'll be able to shake it off as something that you don't need or deserve. If you're really strong, perhaps it will just roll right off of you. And the next time I act like a raging maniac, you can walk out of the room.

PROTAGONIST: How might I learn to live without you?

ANTAGONIST: Obviously, I'm not going anywhere because I get to feel powerful when I get under your skin. But if you must, you could become so incredibly involved with your own happy life that you don't need me. And then, you could just slowly disappear from my life only calling on birthdays.

PROTAGONIST: I'll take that under advisement. Thank you for sharing.

THE PROTAGONIST'S BLESSING

Dear Monica,

I bless you that you should know your own courage, strength, and value, regardless of what anyone says about you. I bless you that you always know you deserve to be treated with love and respect and to not put up with or settle for anything less. I bless you that you should not take on other people's issues as your own. And I bless you that you should never let anyone ever rain on your parade!

CHAPTER THIRTEEN

FALLING ACTION: GETTING THE CLOSURE YOU NEED

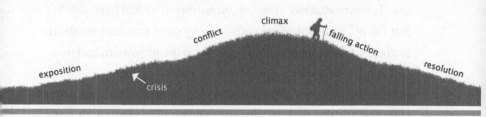

Too often we misunderstand [endings], confuse them with finality — that's it, all over, finished! Yet how we recognize endings is the key to how we can begin anew.

— William Bridges, *Transitions*

Falling Action: The events that transpire following the climax as the story winds down, approaching resolution.

Once the epic battle between the protagonist and the antagonist has transpired, the story begins to wind down toward its inevitable resolution. If you're a little exhausted after completing your climax exercises, then you know exactly how the protagonist feels at this stage of the story. By now, most of the tension has been squeezed out of the plot, and only minor residue remains to be mopped up. The hero returns from battle and reunites with loved ones. The villain is put on trial, or the town begins to clear the debris after the storm. Not surprisingly, we call this part of the story "falling action."

Because it follows the climax, falling action can often be a time of reflection, when the main character, having taken in the view from the summit of the story, begins to tie up loose ends as he or she sees a resolution within sight. After all, after the climactic confrontation or action, your metaphorical hero doesn't just fall off a metaphorical cliff — story over, problem resolved. Rather, it takes time to climb back down the mountain, and there still may be some rocky and steep terrain to negotiate.

The outer story of falling action is all about the events that transpire on the path to closure and the next chapter of your story. Maybe you had the dreaded break-up conversation with your live-in significant other, but before you move out, you've got to figure out how to get your stuff out of the apartment and, perhaps, negotiate the new terms of your continuing relationship. Or maybe you landed your dream job, but now you've got to quit your current one: How will you tell your boss you're leaving and wrap up your projects?

The inner story is about the process of coming to terms with what has unfolded. To achieve closure, we must be willing to let go of, on some level, the primary conflict in our narrative. Letting go often takes time, emotional energy, and perhaps some additional dialogue. In his groundbreaking 1980s book *Transitions*, William Bridges notes that "endings" generally require five fundamental tasks: disengagement (separation from the familiar), dismantling (letting of what is no longer needed), disenchantment (discovering that certain things no longer make sense), disidentification (reevaluating one's identity), and disorientation (a vague sense of losing touch with one's reality). Writes Bridges: "Divorces, deaths, job changes, moves, illnesses, and many lesser events disengage us from the contexts in which we have known ourselves. They break up the old cue system that served to reinforce our roles and pattern our behavior."[24]

Depending on the situation, the path to closure can be emotional as one comes to terms with the gravity of events. For example, after a couple decides to split up, each person can experience anticipatory grief, cycling through waves of sadness, anger, denial, doubt, and acceptance. The couple typically still has a lot to talk about — both to process the events of the "climax" (when you decided to break up) and to prepare for the "resolution" (when you have actually moved out and moved on). The following exercises are designed to help you consider what the protagonist needs in order to get closure.

Closure Exercise

Answer the following questions in the third-person narrative:

1. If the protagonist is still holding on to aspects of the conflict with the antagonist, how might he or she get a sense of closure? What conversations still need to be had? What needs to be grieved?

2. What does disengagement, dismantling, and disidentification look like in the protagonist's chapter narrative?

3. To what degree does the hero experience a sense of disorientation or disenchantment?

4. If you wish, write a dialogue between the protagonist and antagonist that expresses anything that still needs to be said.

Envisioning Your Happy Ending Exercise

Another way to come to terms with the fallout after the climax is to imagine the ideal resolution. This can help you get clarity about what you need to do to best complete the story you're writing and "end" this current chapter of your life. According to motivational guru Stephen Covey, author of the bestselling book *The Seven Habits of Highly Successful People*,[25] when we "begin with the end in mind," we increase the chances of achieving our goals. By imagining our optimum outcome, we can create a mental guide that informs the steps we take to achieve our desired ends. Yes, forces beyond our control can affect the resolution of our story. We might encounter unforeseen obstacles. But we need not choose our paths blindly. Rather, by beginning with the end in mind, we can create a compass in our minds, identify our North Star, and follow our vision to liberation.

Step 1: Write an Inspiring Resolution

Write the resolution, in the third-person narrative, as a story, one that leaves you feeling inspired. Be sure to include aspects of both the outer story (what would actually happen) and the inner story (how the hero would feel about the events that transpire).

Example: Lisa Moves On

In chapter 12, I told Lisa's story and shared the writing she did as she prepared to break up with her longtime boyfriend (see "Envisioning the Climax: Lisa's Breakup," page 154). After Lisa broke up with her boyfriend, there were many tearful nights, uncomfortable moments, and arguments that transpired over the following weeks. Neither of them was ready to let go, and Lisa felt confused. So Lisa wrote the following imagined resolution to her story, which began by describing real events — as she was packing to get ready for her move from New York to Seattle. This exercise helped her realize that, though letting go of Alex was difficult, it was what she needed to do:

Shortly after breaking up with Alex, Lisa starts packing up her stuff. Alex occasionally helps — he's always been so much more organized when it comes to these kinds of things — for which she is grateful. There are many tearful moments, and a few arguments, where he suddenly gets angry with her about something that seems trivial. He seems to be working later than usual, staying away from the apartment, perhaps because it's too painful for him to see her leaving. When the day comes, they embrace each other in a long, heartfelt hug. They tell each other they love each other and will always be there for each other. He wishes her luck. Although she is incredibly sad, she feels at peace with her decision. It feels right. In moments when she isn't grieving her relationship and New York, or feeling anxious about moving to a big city where she only knows a cousin, she's actually pretty excited. She hasn't felt this free in a long time, and the freedom feels really good. She can breathe deeper and even her sleep has improved.

Lisa eventually moves to Seattle, where she thrives at her new job. She makes new friends at work and reconnects with her cousin, who introduces her to all his really cute single friends. She and Alex continue to remain in touch — at first, texting daily. But then the frequency of messages starts to recede. She is okay with this. In fact, she feels

*complete clarity that she made a good choice. She knows
that their lapse in regular interactions is not forever (plus,
she can see what he's up to on Facebook — she is happy he
doesn't unfriend her). He will always hold a special place
in her heart, and she is confident that they will see each
other the next time she visits New York.*

Step 2: Bring Your Resolution to Life

When you've finished writing the imagined resolution, consider how you might bring this story to life, so to speak, so it comes true. Answer the following questions in the third-person narrative, which can help you end your current chapter on a positive note:

1. How might the protagonist apply one or more character strengths — either that the person already possesses or aspires to cultivate — to help improve the chances of achieving the desired resolution? For example, if the strengths are courage and confidence, what would the protagonist do or say that would make him or her feel courageous and confident?
2. How might the hero marshal supporting characters and other resources to manifest this resolution?

CHAPTER FOURTEEN

RESOLUTION: FINDING THE SILVER-LINING NARRATIVE

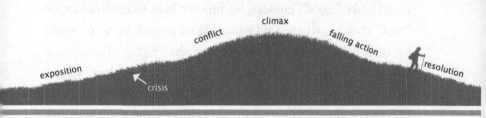

Wherever my story takes me, however dark and difficult the theme, there is always some hope and redemption, not because readers like happy endings, but because I am an optimist at heart. I know the sun will rise in the morning, that there is a light at the end of every tunnel.

— Michael Morpurgo, author of *War Horse*,
quoted in an interview in *The Guardian*

Resolution: The aftermath of the conflict, when stock is taken and the story ends.

When I was young, one of my favorite books was *Sugarcane Island*, which was the first "choose your own adventure" type of interactive book.[26] The premise of *Sugarcane Island* was fairly simple: You had been shipwrecked on a deserted and dangerous island. The goal was survival and finding your way home. At the end of each chapter was a list of possible choices. Whichever one you chose determined your fate in the next chapter.

The problem with the "choose your own adventure" stories was, although the story could end in one of many possible scenarios, I always felt a lot of anxiety. In *Sugarcane Island*, I could make "good" choices, leading me back to civilization, or "bad" choices, where I'd be swallowed by quicksand or eaten by cannibals. Obsessed with making the "right" choice, so I wouldn't wind up on an island native's dinner plate, I read ahead and memorized all the decisions that got me back safely. Of course, once I knew all the safe choices, the book got boring, and I moved on to the next story in the series.

Many people live their lives with a similarly anxious, right-wrong mind-set. The promise of childhood and of fairy tales is that we will survive our trials to live happily ever after. But we know not every story ends wrapped in a bow. Faced with constant choices in a precarious world, many people fear making the wrong moves and dooming themselves to a tragic ending, as if there were only two possible resolutions to every conflict and story. The problem with this thinking is that success is defined narrowly based on a limited set of criteria — in essence, do you get off the island or don't you? In addition, each result is interpreted the same way: getting off the island is always right, and staying is always wrong. But life is rarely this cut-and-dried, and our perspective can change how we regard what happens. Had my sojourn on Sugarcane Island been framed as a learning opportunity, I might not have been so worried about "getting it right." For instance, what if I had been asked to assess what important life lessons I had gleaned or survival skills I had accrued from each choice, or even been presented with the option of writing my own ending? Perhaps I might have even considered remaining on the island a "right" ending — if that meant befriending the natives or establishing a peaceful coexistence with them.

While everyone naturally seeks happy endings, we can't always control the plotline of our story adventure. Even if events unfold in unexpected or undesirable ways, we can still mine our stories for a silver lining, identifying enriching experiences and important lessons to carry into the future.

At the beginning of this book, I stressed the power of interpretation and reclaiming your personal narrative. I offered the anecdote about caring for my father to illustrate that how we spin a tale, and what words we choose and what aspects of a story we focus on, can transform a difficult life chapter into an empowering and uplifting narrative, affecting our sense of fulfillment and satisfaction. Here, at the resolution of your story, you have a powerful opportunity to exercise your authorship rights as you contemplate the meaning of your most recent chapter, reflecting on personal growth, themes, and the underlying moral.

The resolution of a story is the outcome of the conflict between the protagonist and the antagonist. It is the aftermath of the storm, when the clouds have scattered, the dust has settled, and stock is taken. Dorothy discovers that she has always had the power to return home, but she had to find it for herself. She returns to Kansas with a renewed appreciation for family and friendship and a newfound faith in her ability to face her fears.

If we accept the notion that the conflict of our story is a character development workout, the resolution of our story offers us an opportunity to reflect on how much, and in what ways, the protagonist has grown. Whatever happened, was the protagonist successful in strengthening his or her emotional muscles, in both small and significant ways? What did he or she learn? Approaching the resolution of our story, we might also take stock, reflecting on the protagonist's successes and difficulties navigating the story's main conflict. Was the protagonist able to marshal all the gifts and resources at his or her disposal? If not, what got in the way? What dialogues might we still need to imagine in order to let go and move forward? What lessons might we carry into our life's next chapter?

Answers to such powerful questions can help us reframe our story as a personal growth narrative. Instead of seeing a difficult episode in our lives as an unnecessary waste of time, or beating ourselves up for perceived mistakes, we can appreciate the progress we made, even if it's just getting to know ourselves more deeply. This can help us be kinder and gentler with ourselves, leaving us with a more optimistic outlook for the future.

As you approach the resolution of your chapter narrative, reflect on where you've been, how far you've come, what you're still holding on to, and which gifts you might choose to carry into the next chapter of our story.

Finding the Silver-Lining Narrative Exercise

Once the conflict or climax is over (either in real life or only imagined), reflect on what has been resolved and on the protagonist's growth. Write a description of the resolution in the third-person narrative as if it were a story (and not an explanation). When you're done, review it and imagine that it is about a fictional character for whom you feel compassion. Ask the following questions:

1. What emotional muscles, if any, have been strengthened? What growing edges (as identified in chapter 10), were cultivated as a result of this experience?

2. How successful was the protagonist in marshaling strengths, supporting characters, resources, motifs, and learned lessons? Explain.

4. What might the protagonist have done differently, if anything?

5. What lessons and new scripts from this experience might the protagonist choose to carry into the future?

6. Often when a chapter ends, the grief is just beginning. What still needs to be grieved, if anything? Explain.

And the Moral of the Story Is...

Have you ever walked away from a relationship or other significant experience and wondered what it was all about? However, as time passed and emotions settled, you suddenly understood the lesson you were meant to learn that made it all worthwhile. Perhaps you discovered that "love conquers all," "honesty is the best policy," or that you should "never give up on your dreams." Knowingly or unknowingly, you were reaching for the theme or moral of the story.

Themes are the central ideas or messages of a narrative. If our current chapter were a song, themes would be the chorus. Sometimes themes are morals, and sometimes they are ideas about human nature — like love, compassion, fidelity, courage, and trust — that speak to the heart of certain experiences. Essentially, themes are the messages the universe seems to be sending us over and over again: *Trust yourself. Be brave. Sacrifice. Stand up for yourself. Things aren't always what they appear to be.*

While themes may reveal themselves early in the narrative, they are most easily identified toward the end of a story — or life chapter, for our purposes — when the meaning of the plot, the motivations of the characters, and the dynamics of the conflict are clearer and better understood.

The power of identifying the themes and morals is that they help you find redemptive meaning in experiences — take-away lessons to be used in future life chapters — whether or not your story unfolds according to your hopes and expectations. From the vantage point of the resolution, you can measure the value of a particular life episode based on the degree to which you grew and successfully mined it for gems of hard-earned wisdom and experience.

For example, suppose a woman has difficulty expressing her feelings in relationships, fearing judgment and rejection. Recognizing her growing edge as courage and self-expression, she meets someone and decides to practice expressing her thoughts and feelings in appropriate moments. The relationship lasts two years, during which she achieves a level of safety and emotional intimacy that she hadn't experienced before. For other reasons, however, the couple decides that they are not right for each other, and they agree to part ways. She could walk away, dismissing the experience as a waste of time. Alternatively, she could embrace the important lessons — that trust builds intimacy, and that growing close to another human being is valuable regardless of whether it leads to a long-term commitment.

Keep in mind that one storyline may have several themes, both major and minor. Major themes are recurring ideas that appear throughout a life or a novel. Minor themes are ideas that appear periodically, sometimes only in one chapter or a section of the book. For example, a major theme of *Step Out of Your Story* is empowerment through storytelling, while a minor theme is growing through challenges with your antagonist.

Second, discovering common themes can help you shed light on what you truly value.[27] Take Jim's story. Jim was a beloved fifty-six-year-old husband and father of three who saw the glass as half-full. Although his office job offered security and a steady paycheck in a recession, he dreaded going to work, wishing he could do something more creative and lucrative. When he suffered a heart attack, Jim reassessed his priorities and perspective. As he sought alternative sources of income, he also appreciated his family more and took pride in his role as a provider. To satisfy his creativity, he started blogging about his sons. Recurring themes in his life were sacrifice, the importance of family, and personal power.

Or consider Barbara: A fifty-eight-year-old divorced woman, she often defined herself by her ability to sacrifice for others. While her selfless tendencies had served her well when she was raising her children, and later caring for her aging father, she often paid little attention to her own interests and needs. When her father passed and her health began to suffer, Barbara experienced an identity crisis. Though she had many talents, she struggled with the thought of putting herself first. The theme of her chapter was "self-discovery" and "reclaiming her gifts."

Finally, recognizing themes can help us identify our spiritual homework, so to speak, for the current chapter or the larger story of our life. By spiritual homework, I mean the personal growth assignments that seem to be presented to us, over and over again, by a recurring type of antagonist in our story. Perhaps you grew up with a domineering father and tend to find yourself in situations with domineering bosses. Learning to respect yourself even in the absence of external validation, not taking other people's behavior so personally, or embracing your power to leave situations that make you unhappy may be ongoing life lessons that are intrinsically valuable.

The moral of the story, so to speak, is that life is both the meaning we make from it and the lessons we take from it. According to positive psychologists, who study the science of happiness, the more you can find the silver-lining narrative in whatever circumstances you face, the more content you will be. By shedding light on your deepest values and offering lasting lessons, themes can serve as a compass through dark and uncertain times into a happier and more satisfying future.

Theme and Moral Exercise

Take a moment to reflect on some of the major themes in the chart below. These are just some examples — it's not a complete list.

As you do, ask yourself the following questions:

1. What is the major theme in the current chapter you have been exploring? How does this theme fit into the larger story of the protagonist's life? Explain.
2. What is the moral or lesson to be learned? What is the protagonist's spiritual homework? Explain.
3. If your life had a soundtrack, what might be the theme song? Imagine you're editing a movie about

your life, and you've been asked to place this theme song in a recent scene. Where would you place it and why? Describe the scene in the third-person narrative. What do you see and what do you hear? What do you want the audience to feel?

Common Story Themes

This list of common themes in literature may or may not apply to your own story.[28] Use them as inspiration; many participants in my workshops find that examples help them home in on their own themes.

Beauty of simplicity
Change versus tradition
Chaos and order
Circle of life
Coming of age
Companionship as salvation
Convention and rebellion
Dangers of ignorance
Death — inevitable or tragic
Desire to escape
Destruction of beauty
Disillusionment and dreams
Empowerment
Emptiness of

attaining false dreams
Everlasting love
Facing darkness
Facing reality
Fading beauty
Faith versus doubt
Family — blessing or curse
Fate versus free will
Fear of failure
Good versus evil
Greed as downfall
Growing up — pain or pleasure
Hazards of passing judgment
Heartbreak of betrayal
Heroism — real and perceived

Illusion of power
Individual versus society
Inner versus outer strength
Injustice
Knowledge versus ignorance
Letting go
Loneliness as destructive force
Losing hope
Loss of innocence
Lost honor
Lost love
Love and sacrifice
Manipulation
Materialism as downfall
Motherhood
Murphy's law

Nationalism —
  complications
Nature as beauty
Necessity of work
Oppression of
  women
Optimism — power
  or folly
Overcoming —
  fear, weakness,
  vice
Patriotism —
  positive side or
  complications
Power and
  corruption
Power of nature
Power of wealth

Power of words
Pride and
  downfall
Progress — real or
  illusion
Quest for
  immortality
Quest for power
Rebirth
Role of Religion
  — virtue or
  hypocrisy
Self-discovery
Self-reliance
Social mobility
Technology in
  society — good
  or bad

Temptation and
  destruction
Triumph over
  adversity
Vanity as downfall
Vulnerability of the
  meek
Vulnerability of the
  strong
War — glory,
  necessity, pain,
  tragedy
Will to survive
Wisdom of
  experience
Working-class
  struggles
Youth and beauty

CHAPTER FIFTEEN

EPILOGUE: IMAGINING WHAT'S NEXT

I've always been dubious of Hollywood and fairy-tale endings. We never see Prince Charming fight with Cinderella about leaving her shoes all over the house, nor do we find out what happens when Auntie Em dies of breast cancer and the tedium of farm life stirs twenty-year-old Dorothy to catch the next tornado express out of Kansas.

Like life, every story continues or has loose ends, and epilogues tie up these narrative threads, usually for no other reason than to satisfy the reader's curiosity about what happens next. The epilogue might describe what happens weeks, months, or years after the story's resolution, especially in romances, where readers want to know who married whom and what they named their babies.

The epilogue isn't part of the classic story arc but takes place after its completion. Not all stories have epilogues, and a story can end satisfactorily without one. Yet envisioning the epilogue, or the next chapter of our story, can be extremely beneficial. Having reflected on where we've been and where we are, we can now think about where we would like to be headed.

Samantha's Story: No Joking Around

When she first came to see me, twenty-five-year-old Samantha described herself as suffering from "post-traumatic boss disorder." After graduating from a liberal arts college, her dream was to work in comedy as a writer or actress. However, the first decently paying job she found was in a software company, so she took it, even though she had no real experience or long-term interest in it. When her boss proved to be an abusive, domineering control freak, Samantha jumped at the first opportunity to escape, only to find herself at another dead-end job with another crazy boss. She was so miserable that she spent every waking moment of her limited free time exploring how she might break into comedy, taking improv classes and freelancing as a social media writer. Yet she continued to receive one rejection letter after another, leaving her despondent.

Imagining herself as a character in a story, Samantha saw that circumstances were forcing her to push herself beyond her fears of not being good enough to do the one thing that would make her happy — write. Yet, she continued to be plagued by doubts and fears, such as not being able to repay her college loans. In one session together, I gave her a homework assignment to write the next chapter of her life, or the epilogue to our work together, in the third-person narrative. When she returned the following week, Samantha confessed she found it difficult. With so many possibilities, she wasn't sure if she should write her dream life or the most realistic scenario, and she was worried about jinxing her future. I asked her to try the exercise again, only this time to focus on how she wanted to feel about her job in the next chapter. This freed her up to explore her future with broader strokes, focusing on her growing edges of "confidence" and "self-trust":

> *In the next chapter, Samantha will feel like she is moving closer and closer to transitioning to a career in a creative field. When people ask what she does for a living, she will feel proud to tell them. Even if it's not exactly what she wants to be doing, she will feel good about the experience she is getting, knowing it will help propel her toward her goals. Samantha will be confident in her abilities and judgments, using her creativity to turn yesterday's trash into tomorrow's treasure. Her growing trust in herself will ripple into other areas of her life, helping her make important decisions in her relationships and career.*

Because epilogues give us a window into the protagonist's future, I invite you to complete one last writing exercise now that you've considered the resolution of your current chapter. In real life, our epilogues are not really endings but rather the beginnings of the next chapter or story. Consequently, the story of our lives is more like a spiral than a bell curve. With each circular revolution, we approach familiar themes with the wisdom we have acquired from previous episodes. The spiral continues circling, transporting us to new heights.

Epilogue Exercise

The Epilogue Exercise is designed to help you consider where your protagonist is headed and how he or she might arrive safely and in good spirits. Please be sure to complete the following exercise in the third-person narrative, writing as if telling a story (not answering the questions with explanations). Note that this exercise isn't meant to address the current chapter and it's main conflict; instead, write the epilogue like the beginning of the next chapter, imagining events to come:

1. What will or might the next chapter of the protagonist's life be about? Write a brief description of this next chapter and give it a title.
2. Include in this epilogue how the protagonist will feel about him or herself, including about relationships, career, and other important aspects of his or her life.
3. What steps could the protagonist take now to move the story forward? Include these in the epilogue as well.

CHAPTER SIXTEEN

STEP BACK INTO YOUR STORY

I'd like to suggest an alternative "success" story — one where with each next, the protagonist is closer to finding that spot where he's no longer held back by his heart, and he explodes with talent, and his character blossoms, and the gift he has to offer the world is apparent.

— Po Bronson, *What Should I Do with My Life?*

Throughout this process I've asked you to step out of your usual way of seeing things to get a novel perspective on a familiar story — your own. Perhaps you've discovered your inner superhero or had an "aha" moment about historically self-defeating behaviors. Hopefully, you now perceive your life through a more compassionate lens and have gained new insights into motivations, themes, and antagonizing forces shaping your storyline.

185

Having completed this process once, you have all the pieces you need to continue creating new stories about where you are in your life and where you're going. At the beginning of this journey, you performed a character sketch in which you identified, among other things, the values, desires, blocks, and stakes involved in the choices facing you at this juncture in your story. You also identified the outmoded roles and scripts that were getting in the way of living your best life.

Then, focusing on the current chapter of your life, you looked at how your primary antagonist was helping you become a more complete, fully expressed version of yourself by pushing you to muster your strengths, identify your vulnerabilities, and work toward your growing edges. You also explored how marshaling your supporting characters and resources could help you overcome obstacles.

You also imagined and anticipated the climax of your story, the much-anticipated confrontation with your antagonist. Whether this unfolded only through imagined dialogue or also in real life, you then reflected on how this conflict resolved, mining it for important lessons and themes. Finally, you envisioned what the next chapter of your narrative might look like.

Now it's time to step back into your story and reclaim your personal narrative. In the next exercise, we will weave together the threads of insight from each chapter into a cohesive new narrative.

However, instead of using the third-person narrative, I'd like you to reembody your narrative using the *first-person* voice. Why switch voices? Remember, the purpose of writing in the third person is to create some emotional distance between you and your inner critic so that your higher self will be free to explore your story from a novel perspective. Now that you've done this, it's time to reenter your story. The first-person voice is intimate and primal. It's how we speak directly about ourselves, using "I," "me," and "mine." Retelling your new story in a far more personal voice will help you integrate this new lens into your larger personal narrative. It's as if you have returned home after taking a trip. Now it's time to unpack your bags and arrange your souvenirs around the house, fitting the new Tuscan-style pottery you bought next to the terra-cotta vase you purchased in Santa Fe last year. You need to integrate the keepsakes of your journey into your existing personal décor — to make it yours.

When you're done, consider keeping this new version of your story where you can see it or access it easily. Tack this exercise to your refrigerator or slip it inside a journal and use it like a compass, keeping you on track and moving in the right direction as you navigate the shifting currents of your life.

Reconstructing Your Story Exercise

In your journal or on a separate sheet, please complete this exercise in the first-person narrative. Prompts below the lines signal what to write. This exercise summarizes all of the story writing and exercises into a descriptive essay.

Exposition

The current chapter of my life: _____

[Title]

is about: _____

[Chapter description combining aspects of character sketch]

Some defining moments of this chapter have been:

_____

[Outer story]

These events have affected me in the following ways:

_____

[Inner story]

Conflict

One of my biggest challenges right now is: _____

[Primary antagonist]

I struggle with this challenge because it brings up my
    tendency to: _____

[Describe vulnerabilities]

Still, I can see this challenge as helping me to cultivate:

_____

[Character strengths and growing edges]

My strengths, which include: _____

and my resources, such as: _____

help me navigate these challenges, which I am actively transforming into personal growth opportunities by shifting my perspective.

_____

[Supporting characters]

also provide me with encouragement and support.

Climax

This chapter may reach/reaches a climax when: _____

_____

[Climax]

at which time I realize: _____

[Epiphany]

Resolution

It is ultimately resolved when: _____

[Resolution]

During this time, I notice the following morals and themes: _____

[Themes]

The moral of the story appears to be: _____

[Moral]

In the next chapter: _____

[Title]

I will focus on: _____

[Synopsis of epilogue]

CHAPTER SEVENTEEN

YOUR WORK IN PROGRESS

Now that you understand how to use your story glasses, you can use them to explore the larger story of your life. Of course, the question "What is the story of my life about?" defies easy answers. Throughout our lifetime, our narrative is always changing. Our autobiography at age thirty will be different than at age sixty, probably with a different title, antagonist, and conflict. Still, regardless of our age, we benefit from viewing the various chapters of our life through the lens and framework of storytelling, identifying the primary antagonists, themes, and lessons that keep showing up in our narrative.

This chapter presents a chart that offers a "novel perspective" on your entire life story. The chart guides you in creating what is essentially a condensed "plot outline" that summarizes each chapter in your life so far, using this book's terms. This will give you a sweeping view of your narrative and a chance to observe your protagonist's character development over the course of your life — or over the course of the whole novel, so to speak, and not just the current chapter. Looking at the larger tapestry of your life, you can begin to weave the seemingly fragmented chapters of your story into a meaningful narrative that values the subtle, often unrecognized personal victories that build character.

Before you begin, however, please keep a few things in mind. First, in the chart, each chapter prompts you to summarize one decade, more or less. I chose decades simply because it's the easiest and most logical way to bookend a period of time. Still, these periods may not reflect the best chapter divisions for your life; indeed, stages of life rarely wrap themselves up in neat ten-year packages. As such, feel free to change the dates and time span of each chapter when you make your own chart, creating more personally meaningful increments.

As you're completing the chart, and especially if you're organizing by decade, try not to get hung up on whether or not you have achieved certain age-associated milestones. I find that many of my clients, particularly those in their thirties and forties, have unrealistic checklists of accomplishments they believe they should have reached by a certain age — a happy marriage, a house, children, career success, and so on. If there's a store that sells these checklists, it's doing a phenomenal marketing job. Not only does everyone seem to have the same list, they make the same assumptions — that everyone else has more checkmarks than they do, and that the more checks you have, the happier you will be.

I don't buy such checklists. They're deceiving. People are a lot like plants; they flourish and bloom at different times and under individually favorable conditions. Many factors influence someone's personal evolution — parenting, genetics, culture, and the things that happen to them. It's important to remember that personal growth is not a race to be the first to fulfill societal expectations or achieve certain milestones — it's a lifelong organic process. In fact, renowned Swiss psychologist Carl Jung held that becoming one's own person was the primary goal of human development.

In other words, if you think you're not where you should be, don't beat yourself up. Rather, consider adopting the rubric of my former dance teacher, who used to say, "It's not worth comparing yourself to others. There will always be people better than you and worse than you. The most important thing is to ask yourself, 'Am I improving?'"

This is the ultimate point of this book, and one that I hope you continue to reflect on at every point in your journey. For efficiency's sake, try to opt for longer time spans (like three to twelve years). You can either fold the current chapter narrative you already completed into one of the longer chapters, or keep it separate, as long as you don't mind if your chart is a bit uneven, with one chapter shorter than the rest. That aside, this is your story. You can write it your way.

My Life Story Exercise

For this exercise, create your own chart based on the one here. You can either use a large sheet of poster board or a Word/Excel document. Each of these approaches has its advantages and disadvantages:

- If you are technologically proficient, the latter option is preferred, as you can easily create a table that resembles the one in this book. Use the "landscape"

MY LIFE STORY

Timeline (age range)	Chapter Title	Plot Summary (see chapter 6): What happened during this time period? What were the major adjustments?	Conflict (see chapters 8 and 9): Who or what were your major antagonists? What kinds of personal challenges did you experience?	Supporting Characters and Resources (see chapter 11): Who played a supportive role in your story? What other support and resources were available?
0–12				
13–21				
22–30				
31–40				
41–50				
51–60				
61–70				
71–80 (and so on)				

	Climax (see chapter 12): What were the highlights of this time in your life? This might include proud moments or turning points.	Resolution (see chapters 13 and 14): How did you resolve the "conflict"?	Character Development (see chapter 10): What strengths did you cultivate as a result of this experience?

page format. If you're unsure how to create a table in Word or Excel and have no idea what "landscape" means, choose one of the following alternatives.

- If you are more artistically inclined, and like using felt-tip, colored markers, create your chart on a large piece of poster board. The advantage of using poster board is that you could also decorate your chart, drawing images to represent different chapters of your life. If you really want to go wild, you can use photographs, stickers, glitter, and other artistic flourishes to round out your living story.

- Of course, you can also use a large notebook, with either graph or lined paper, for a neater presentation. If you prefer to write this in your journal and don't have enough space for the full chart, disregard the table and use one or two pages to describe each chapter. If you feel so inclined, you can unpack them discursively. But be sure to include all the story elements encompassed in the table, perhaps beginning with an outline.

Once again, the decades in the chart below are intended as suggested benchmarks. Feel free to divide your life story into consecutive periods of time that make more sense to you (up to, say, twenty years). You can get creative as long as each chapter, representing a discrete time period, contains all the story parameters we've covered in this book, particularly a set of challenges you faced, both positive and negative, that changed you in some way. For each story element, I've provided book chapter references in case you need to review. You might consider breaking down your chapters according to the following elements of the story, some of which will overlap, depending on the title you give to your chapter:

ROLES: The predominant roles of your life — for example, daughter, college student, young professional, working mother, empty nester, retiree, and so on. You might call a chapter "Supermom" or "Empty Nesting."

SETTING: Places you have lived or discrete periods of time that have meaning for you. For example, "Baltimore Days" or "Life on Campus."

THEMES: Dominant themes such as "Loss of Innocence," "Falling in Love," "Building a Family," or "Reinventing Myself."

For this exercise, you can use whatever narrative voice feels right to you — either first or third person. I encourage you to write in an abbreviated fashion — no need to write complete sentences or explanations. Shorthand is acceptable. When you've completed your chart or outline, answer the questions in the "Reflecting on Your Life Story Exercise" below. After reflecting on the chart, you may discover a chapter that feels unresolved; in other words, you haven't made peace with it yet. Perhaps it never reached its climax or maybe the resolution didn't feel satisfying. If this rings true, complete the optional "Rewriting Unresolved Chapters Exercise" that concludes the book.

Reflecting on Your Life Story Exercise

1. Suppose you published your memoir or autobiography. What would the title be, and how might it be described on the back cover blurb?

2. When you examine the story of your life, what stands out and why?

3. Do you notice any patterns? For example, do similar kinds of conflicts keep emerging, or has a particular strength been repeatedly helpful in working through conflicts?

4. Are there chapters in your life of which you are particularly proud? Explain.

5. What has helped you transition from one chapter to the next? (For example, do you remember an experience in which you realized you were no longer a child; what signaled your maturity?)

6. What has been the climax of your life up to this point? Describe the chapter and why you selected it. Why do you consider this is the climax of the story? As the story continues, can you imagine another climax? What might it look like?

7. In what ways have poorly written scripts prevented you from fulfilling your potential? What were those scripts, and how might you rewrite them?

8. What is heroic about your journey?

Rewriting Unresolved Chapters Exercise

If you feel that one or more chapters in your life story are unresolved, consider writing a description of those chapters in the third-person narrative, using the lessons throughout this book to make meaning of these episodes. Feel free to apply any of the writing exercises from the book, or simply answer the following questions, as they apply:

1. Describe the protagonist, in the third-person narrative, as he or she appeared in that chapter. What was his or her motivation? What was his or her obstacle? What was at stake?

2. Describe the antagonist.

3. What character strengths did the protagonist develop as a result of his or her interactions with the antagonist?

4. What old scripts and roles keep interfering with the protagonist's ability to actualize his or her best self?

5. What new roles and scripts might he or she embrace to stop the cycle?

6. How might you reframe the chapter narrative so that you imagined the protagonist overcoming a significant obstacle or learning something valuable?

7. Rewrite the chapter summary from a novel perspective, applying the tools and lessons you've learned on our journey together. Identify the redemptive, silver-lining narrative.

The Yellow Brick Road Continues

Congratulations. We've reached the end of this book, but not the end of your story. After all, every conclusion is ultimately the backstory of a brand new narrative. So long as we are alive, we continue to grow. And so long as we grow, there will always be plot twists and antagonists, benevolent and otherwise, pushing us to step out our comfort zones and more deeply into the characters we play. I hope you have discovered a helpful framework for looking at life, and that you will continue to apply the lessons and insights of this journey to your ever-evolving story, returning to your favorite exercises when you are stuck or need a fresh perspective. But for now, may you continue to make story alchemy, mining the redemptive narrative hidden in the subtext of every plotline. It's always there if you are willing to step out of your story.

ACKNOWLEDGMENTS

Every book has a story behind it, and every story is a transformational journey. As both author and protagonist of this book, I am grateful to the many supporting characters who helped me grow into the sort of character who could write a book. They include, but are not limited to, the following:

To my clients and writing students who entrusted me with their stories. I feel blessed to serve as both witness and midwife to your growth and transformation. Without you, there would be no book. I'm particularly indebted to Gavriel Meir Levy, who envisioned my workshop as a workbook, and for Ellen Spector-Haighney, Cindyanne Rabinowitz, and other students at my 92nd Street Y "Writing from the Novel Perspective" workshop, who encouraged me to begin writing it.

To Janet Rosen, my devoted agent at Sheree Bykofsky Associates, who recognized the book's potential and helped shepherd this work into the world. Thanks, as well, for managing my expectations and offering words of reassurance through the entire arc of the publishing process, including both peaks and valleys. To Georgia Hughes, my editor at New World Library, for her many talents, editorial insight, formidable patience, hours of labor, and abiding faith in the promise of this book. I am especially grateful to Georgia and the staff at New World Library for taking a chance on me and keeping the faith.

To the best supporting characters an author/protagonist could ask for: Jory Stillman, Paige Betten, Rebecca Schweiger, Jamie Askin, Yiska Obadia, Sam Gedal, Sean Shannon, Beverly Pincus, Ranai Freedman, Allegra Kochman, David Kaufman, Sharon Dolin, Howard Wiener, Wendy Morris, Shoshana Shamberg, Rachel Kraft Elliot, Dana Hartman, and Eileen Arsenault. Thank you for believing in me, indulging my occasional fix for editorial/design feedback, and for understanding when I couldn't come out and play. I couldn't ask for better friends, and I feel blessed to be on this journey together.

Special thanks to Ken Ross, for being the incredible gift that you are in my life, and for entering at just the right time. Also, to my beloved aunt and soul sister Janis Richman, for her boundless love and depth of devotion to the fulfillment of my dreams and for helping me stay connected to my vision. Love you mucho. And, if ever there was a champion for the book, it was my dear friend and undercover superhero Mark Siegel, who edited earlier versions of the manuscript and rallied me to "step into my power," "embrace my own unique voice," and stop hiding from the "reader." (I've done it, now it's your turn!) While we're on the subject of superheroes, I am deeply grateful to Dominic Dimele, for his exuberant friendship, his financial management, and his inspirational words, songs, and images, and for embodying many of the character virtues described in this book.

And, of course, where would I be without my weekly dose of love, encouragement, inspiration, and wisdom from my beloved soul brothers and sisters at Romemu? I feel so blessed to be part of such a loving community, under the inspired leadership of Rabbi David Ingber, that constantly illuminates the divinity in others and in myself. Also, a special thank you to Rabbi Dianne Cohler-Esses and the "Romemu Adult Education Dream Team" for understanding when I needed to take a step back to focus on the book. Speaking of blessings, I am deeply grateful to Naomi Cohen for helping me embrace my unfolding story with unconditional love and compassion. Thank you, as well, for your insight, encouragement, support, and assistance with prioritizing writing.

Sometimes, small- and medium-size gestures make a huge difference. Which is why I owe a special debt of gratitude to Jane Graver, for her honest, insightful, and provocative feedback on earlier versions and for being a generous hostess during my week-long writing marathon in New Jersey. I'm similarly indebted to David Kaufman, who let me use his family home in Chatham as a writer's retreat to wade through the last round of copyediting. I am equally grateful for my many readers, including Joshua Sussman, Laura Srehnik, Mijanou Mosher, Kitty Hoffman, Mitch Rubenstein, and Andreas Coronas, who helped transition my story platform from workshop to workbook. Whether or not I used your examples, your willingness to act as guinea pigs helped me improve both the exercises and the instructions. I am also indebted to the Hirschorn family for tending to Munchkin while I wrote. To George Brieger and Eric Ackland, for their insightful feedback on earlier edits of the book proposal. Thank you, as well, to Sharon Goldman Wallach who booked my first workshop at the 92nd Street Y.

For seeing me through the last painful contractions of birthing this book, I offer a special thanks to several editors who encouraged me to keep pushing, even though I was, metaphorically speaking, ready for a cesarean. They include PJ Dempsey, who performed the editorial equivalent of turning the baby's head around so that my introduction and first few chapters were leading in the right direction. And to editor and new friend Temma Ehrenfeld, who assured me that I had the makings of a healthy baby book that just needed a good copyeditor. (And to my dear friend Yiska Obadia, a professional baby doula and healer, who rallied me to "keep pushing" despite my exhaustion.) And, of course, for finding and finessing the problem spots, I'm indebted to Jeff Campbell, copy editor extraordinaire. Also, thank you Tracy Cunningham and Tona Pearce Myers at New World Library for creating such warm and inviting pages and a cover that complements the book so nicely.

To my devoted brother, Brett Schneiderman, whose heartfelt encouragement and support of this project has meant the world to me. To all the uncles and cousins of the Richman and Schneiderman family for their unconditional love and support. A special shout out to Elayne Karp, Jordana Freeman, Robyn Angell, and Ari Schneiderman for weighing in on book titles (a welcome distraction) during my father's Shiva.

Sending gratitude vibrations to my wonderful parents, who planted the seeds of creativity and intelligence but left the world before they could see the book's fruition. Without their undying love, none of this would have been possible. Their contributions to this book are innumerable. And, of course, I am grateful to God, my coauthor, for conspiring to help me write this book in so many miraculous ways.

Finally, a special thanks to anyone I have ever considered an antagonist in my story. Though I may kvetch and protest, in the end, I am a stronger, deeper, wiser, and more compassionate human being because of you.

NOTES

Introduction

1. For an overview of this research, see Michele M. Tugade, Barbara L. Fredrickson, and Lisa Feldman Barrett, "Psychological Resilience and Positive Emotional Granularity: Examining the Benefits of Positive Emotions on Coping and Health," *Journal of Personality* 72, no. 6 (December 2004): 1161–90, http://www.ncbi.nlm.nih.gov /pmc/articles/PMC1201429/.

Chapter One. Embracing the Story Lens on Life

2. For a quick overview of some narrative terms, see John August, "What's the Difference Between a Hero, a Main Character and a Protagonist?" JohnAugust.com, July 26, 2005, http://johnaugust .com/2005/whats-the-difference-between-hero-main-character -and-protagonist.
3. Dan P. McAdams, *The Stories We Live By* (New York: The Guilford Press, 1993), 27, 30.

Chapter Two. Shifting Your Perspective

4. PBS, *This Emotional Life*, episode 2, "Facing Our Fears," January 6, 2010, http://www.pbs.org/thisemotionallife/series/episodes/2.

5. O. Ayduk and E. Kross, "From a Distance: Implications of Spontaneous Self-Distancing for Adaptive Self-Reflection," *Journal of Personality and Social Psychology* 98 (May 2010): 809–29.
6. L. K. Libby, R. P. Eibach, and T. Gilovich, "Here's Looking at Me: The Effect of Memory Perspective on Assessments of Personal Change," *Journal of Personality and Social Psychology* 88 (January 2005): 50–62.
7. E. Kross, O. Ayduk, and W. Mischel, "When Asking 'Why' Does Not Hurt: Distinguishing Rumination from Reflective Processing of Negative Emotions," *Psychological Science* 16 (September 2005): 709–15.
8. PBS, *This Emotional Life.*

Chapter Three. Getting to Know the Star of Your Story

9. McAdams, *Stories We Live By*, 11.
10. Ibid.
11. Anne Lamott, *Bird by Bird: Some Instructions on Writing and Life* (New York: Anchor Books, 1994), 45.
12. This question is from Writeworld.com, "Additional Questions for the Character Questionnaire (By Creative Writing Now)," http://writeworld.org/private/25805127445/tumblr_m654j3vONg1rnl2v3.
13. This question is from Gotham Writers, "Character Questionnaires," http://www.writingclasses.com/InformationPages/index.php/PageID/106.
14. The two "dream" questions are from Writeworld.com, "Additional Questions."

Chapter Six. Naming and Describing Your Chapter

15. Eckhart Tolle, *The Power of Now* (Novato, CA: New World Library, 1999), 50.

Chapter Seven. Doom or Bloom: Exploring the Power of Spin

16. David Ingber, *Turning Straw into Gold: The Power of Narrative*, January 20, 2013, http://dev.romemu.org/sermon/turning-straw-into-gold-the-power-of-narrative/.
17. Wendig, Chuck, "25 Things You Should Know About Protagonists,"

Terrible Minds, February 14, 2012, http://terribleminds.com/ramble/2012/02/14/25-things-you-should-know-about-protagonists/.

18. Betty Smith, *A Tree Grows in Brooklyn* (New York: Harper & Brothers, 1943), 1; Edward Bulwer-Lytton, *Paul Clifford* (Rockville, MD: Wildside Press, 2004), 1.

19. McAdams, *Stories We Live By,* 47.

Chapter Nine. Reading Between the Lines: Exploring Character Strengths and Vulnerabilities

20. Brené Brown, "The Power of Vulnerability," TED Talk, June 2010, www.ted.com/talks/brene_brown_on_vulnerability.

Chapter Ten. Using Dialogue to Mine Your Story and Transform Your Character

21. Tara Brach, *Radical Acceptance* (New York: Bantam Dell, 2003).

Chapter Eleven. Supporting Characters and Other Resources

22. Joseph Campbell, *The Hero with a Thousand Faces* (Novato, CA: New World Library, 1949, 2008).

Chapter Twelve. Climax: As Your Story Turns

23. Rabbi Aryeh Kaplan, *The Living Torah* (New York: Maznaim Publishing Corporation, 1981), 157.

Chapter Thirteen. Falling Action: Getting the Closure You Need

24. William Bridges, *Transitions* (Cambridge, MA: Da Capo Press, 2004), 113.

25. Stephen R. Covey, *The Seven Habits of Highly Successful People* (New York: Simon & Schuster, 1989), 95.

Chapter Fourteen. Resolution: Finding the Silver-Lining Narrative

26. Edward Packard, *Sugarcane Island,* 3rd ed. (New York: Bantam Books, 1986).

27. For more about identifying a theme, see C. A. Dowler, "Looking for Your Life Theme?" Manifest Your Potential.com, 2013, http://www.manifestyourpotential.com/self_discovery/3_discover _your_life_way/life-theme.htm

28. This list of themes is adapted from Grace Fleming, "100 Common Book Themes," About.com, http://homeworktips.about.com/od /writingabookreport/a/themelist.htm.

ABOUT THE AUTHOR

Kim Schneiderman, LCSW, MSW, is a psychotherapist, workshop facilitator, former journalist and adjunct professor, and spiritual essayist who lives and works in New York City. She writes a psychological advice column, "No Insurance Necessary," for the New York, Boston, and Philadelphia *Metro* daily newspapers http://www.metro.us/newyork, which have an aggregate circulation of roughly 4,000,000 readers. She counsels adults through her private psychotherapy practice and has facilitated therapeutic writing groups at the 92nd Street Y, the JCC in Manhattan, FEGS Health and Human Services, the Jewish Board of Family and Children's Services (JBFCS), the Association of Spirituality and Psychotherapy (ASP), Art Studio NY, Limmud New York, and various other venues. She has worked as an adjunct professor for the Long Island University's School of Social Work and served as a Guest Lecturer for New York University's Post-Graduate Social Work and Spiritual Care certificate program, a program she also completed. Ms. Schneiderman has written dozens of freelance articles, including cover stories, for major Jewish newspapers, including *The Jewish Week*, the *Baltimore Jewish Times*, the *Northern California Jewish Bulletin*, and *Aish.com*. Her blog, The Novel Perspective, is popular on the *Psychology Today* website. For more information, visit her website at www.stepoutofyourstory.com.